RedeFIND SiNGLE 40+

RedeFIND 40+
SiNGLE

How to Springboard to a New Life by Redefining & Rediscovering Who You Really Are

CATHERINE GARRETT

iUniverse LLC
Bloomington

RedeFIND SiNGLE 40+
How to Springboard to a New Life by Redefining
& Rediscovering Who You Really Are

iUniverse books may be ordered through booksellers or by contacting:

iUniverse
1663 Liberty Drive
Bloomington, IN 47403
www.iuniverse.com
1-800-Authors (1-800-288-4677)

ISBN: 978-1-4759-9798-9 (sc)
ISBN: 978-1-4759-9800-9 (hc)
ISBN: 978-1-4759-9799-6 (e)

Library of Congress Control Number: 2013915434

Printed in the United States of America.

iUniverse rev. date: 09/09/2013

IN GRATITUDE

RedeFIND SiNGLE 40+ is dedicated to my ex and all the kind people who inspired me to embrace all of who I truly am during the breakup of my marriage.

The relationship with my ex was an enormous contribution to my life. Throughout our twenty years together, I grew from a girl to a woman. Our adventure together assisted me in stepping more fully into who I actually am, and it pressed me to remember my passions. Although throughout this book I share the trials of our relationship, this man's impact on my life was the inspiration I required to see my true genius potential. I am in total appreciation for all that he contributed to my life's journey.

All of the women surrounding me—friends, family, clients, and students—have been a blessing. How did I get lucky enough to attract and surround myself with such incredible energies? Thanks to all of you for believing in me, sharing your stories and aha moments, and allowing me to learn from each of you.

A final and most heartfelt thanks to my lover, Bill, who assisted me throughout the editing and publishing process of this book. We creative types can be somewhat protective of our own work. I adore him!

CONTENTS

PREFACE

One evening, after twenty years of marriage, my husband and I chose to go our separate ways. Our impending separation had been fermenting for years. We were both agitated and tired of being bottled up together, feeling more like roommates than partners. Each of us was ready to release ourselves from the limitations we were causing one another. In the blink of an eye, my life was turned upside down.

My son and I moved to an apartment, and I began my new life as a single woman—and a single mom—over forty. As a life coach, I have shared many techniques and processes to help women remember their passions and live more joyful lives. With my own fears of the unknown looming, I made a conscious decision to redefine my life. What better way, I thought, than to play with all the tools I use to assist my clients?

I started by deliberately focusing on my fears, using techniques I designed, to help me transform fearful emotions into exciting ones. As I began the transference, within me, from fear to the exhilaration of excitement, I felt my body relaxing. The next step was to put an end to my negative self-talk, and I began journal exercises. Writing is an excellent way to release negative emotions and become aware of the limiting definitions, beliefs, and patterns you are fixating on.

I understood the power of putting my story, thoughts, and feelings onto paper. When our thoughts and feelings are in overdrive, popping up and causing constant, unwanted, internal conflicts, we become overwhelmed. Putting them on paper allows us to see them as something tangible that we are able to work with. And so I wrote.

In the beginning, it was not my intention to write a book to be shared with anyone. I was strictly writing as a form of therapy and release for myself. However, I soon found I was sharing more than usual stories and feelings; I was actually writing as though I was encouraging others. In my mind, I saw myself as a class I was motivating. When one of my good friends got her hands on it, she encouraged me to publish—and this book was born.

I've written *RedeFIND SiNGLE 40+* for women over forty who have recently stepped out of a long marriage or relationship and have a desire to create a new, exciting life, remembering who they are. Living as a single woman, later in life, is quite different from being single in your early twenties. Where once you may have accepted that the relationship was over and moved on, now it's not quite that simple. For years you may have been Mrs. So-and-So, Mr. Whatshisname's wife, or a couple; now it's only you.

At one time in your life, you were an individual who had dreams and desires. Do you remember her? So many women cut themselves off from who they truly are in order to fit into a societal group, dictating multitasking as a way to meet family or specific lifestyle needs. They've put their passions at the bottom of their own list of priorities and feel disempowered, unmotivated, and lost in their newfound singledom. As you look back at the events of your life, do you regret not jumping on an opportunity? Are you kicking yourself in the butt for not making different choices? How often has the easy path presented itself—and you simply chose not to do it?

In this book, I'm not going to tell you how to deal with your ex, get your finances in order, change the oil in your car, or fix a leaky faucet. With the processes, exercises, and meditations I share, I will give you an opportunity to redefine, rediscover, and find you again. I ask that you keep an open mind since some of the ideas, concepts, and exercises may be foreign to you. I also encourage you to reread this book three months from now; you will be in a different place emotionally and ready to receive even more ideas and concepts I share. We can only learn what we are ready to learn at any specific time. Sometimes, the best course of action is to play with one area of your life, one circumstance, or one situation—and adopt a whole new perspective. Create some progress in that area and watch the wave ripple into other areas of your life. Hey! It obviously works for the negative stuff we choose to buy into; why not use this creative energy to your advantage? It is my intention to help you do just that.

I know all too well what it's like to be past forty and trying to grasp being on your own after a long relationship. I would like to help you move from viewing this as a scary, disempowering experience to seeing it as one of empowerment, excitement, and joyous anticipation. I'm not a psychologist and will never claim to be one. However, I have studied energy healing techniques such as Reiki, Blue Matrix, Integrated Energy Therapy, and Access Consciousness. I've taken six sensory, medium, dowsing, chakra-clearing, and meditation courses—and I have been living my life according to the teachings of the Law of Attraction—for over ten years.

Known as the KiCKASS iNTUiTIVE Life Coach, I have taught Law of Attraction classes, coached women individually, spoken to groups, hosted teleclasses, and facilitated online telesummits firing up mind-blowing conversations with the most profound thought leaders, coaches, motivators, and spiritual teachers from around the globe. I offer hands-on experience to assist women in unplugging from the limiting realities they have chosen to create—and buy into—and show them how to live an electrifying life by focusing on their passions and strengths.

I invite all single women who have released themselves from long relationships to discover the hidden gems this circumstance has, and is, providing. Although most of the information I have included speaks to women over forty, the tools, techniques, and processes included are not limited to anyone in particular. No matter what your age, you may feel the desire to redefine yourself and adopt a whole new perspective on life. I ask you to summon all your extraordinary feminine powers and unleash yourself on the world. I encourage you to grab hold of your passions, knowing they do, in fact, exist and discover the joy of remembering and redefining who you are. Finally, I ask you to accept being silly, weird, strange, or unusual and be a shining example for others, giving them the courage to do the same.

This planet shares itself with us from all different angles. You are the "allower" of what you wish to see. In all circumstances, you have a choice. I have played many roles in this life: adorable toddler, teenage brat, bossy friend, wicked sister, slutty bar babe, drug abuser, supportive friend, domineering boss, oversensitive lover, savvy artist, spiteful wife, adoring girlfriend, victim, aggressor, teacher, student, and many more. Who we are encompasses more than we can imagine. I believe we are all things, and that at any time throughout our lives, as situations present themselves, we step more fully into who we truly are.

I appreciate the opportunity to share *RedeFIND SiNGLE 40+* with you. I invite you to embrace being on your own at this seasoned age and encourage you to discover how to live life passionately. Imagine the pleasure of learning how to transform the way you think, connect with your body, and embrace your spirit and passions.

Chapter One
EVERYTHING CHANGES IN THE BLINK OF AN EYE

There is a moment ... and its timing is highly unpredictable. Amid the chaos of resolving new living arrangements, bickering over possessions, squabbling while separating finances, and doing your best to keep a lid on the fact that your marriage is over, it presents itself. You could be out walking your dog, making a cup of tea, sending a text message, preparing dinner, or chatting on the phone with your best friend. It's one of those bizarre flashes where, in the blink of an eye, time is frozen and you experience a heightened sense of awareness. In that stillness, your attention turns inward. You relax and release your breath ... ah, there is clarity. The heavy haze of break-up shock lifts for the slightest moment, and one abundantly clear message comes to mind: *I am alone.*

What happens after this moment slips away is an individual experience for every woman. Some let the outside world punch through that stillness and reclaim its space, slipping back into the familiar, wretched brain fog they've become accustomed to. This additional information only adds to their frustrations. Maybe it's as though, in this brief flicker of time, a window has opened. Fresh air sweeps across your face, breathing life into the promise of better experiences to come, a small breather within the mayhem. Did you choose to receive this information and step fully into your new role as a single woman, excited about the possibilities before you? No matter what occurs in this blink of an eye, it is an incredibly precious moment where you have come to another life-altering fork in your road of life. You are standing at an intersection that offers choices. Whether you choose to respond consciously or simply continue to react, you will continue forward with this new insight, unknowingly or not.

Fifteen, twenty, maybe more than thirty years have magically merged into this one instant. Everything you have done, been, seen, and lived has culminated here and now. You are alone. At night, no one is beside you, pressing their body against yours or breathing onto the back of your neck. No one will roll over and hit you with an elbow or steal the sheets. You no longer need to wait for anyone to come home or to schedule a movie night with. A morning chat sipping tea or coffee before beginning your day is no longer an option. It's just you … on your own now.

For many women, the idea of taking over the entire bed sounds inviting. From your perspective, does it feel empty? Errands and responsibilities are yours alone to manage. Washing laundry, grocery shopping, and tending to children or teens who are continuing with you on this part of your life's travels are all up to you. The perspective you bought into during that flash of clarity—whether you chose to move forward or continue to react to your new environment—illustrates how you are feeling right now.

You're Single Again!

That's right, you are single—the thing you were years ago and did everything not to be since you completed high school. In my youth and social circle, girls focused an excessive amount of energy attempting to locate Mr. Right, usually as soon as they stepped into their ninth grade homeroom. Many couldn't even wait this long, claiming boy after boy as their boyfriend throughout public school. We were just babies, but we were already skilled enough socially to know how to charm a young man with our girlish qualities, toy with his emotions, and then dump him and go in search of the next boy to manipulate. Countless women from my generation were trained to keep their eyes peeled for Mr. Right, snatch him, get married, and have babies. The role of our captives was to take care of us, pamper us whenever possible, and keep us safe.

As seasoned women now, we find ourselves once again mixed up in this crazy game of cat and mouse. For those of us who have decided that living alone is not an option, we usually go on the prowl for Mr. Right, using the same methods we employed in our youth. Many of us crave this perfect man who will fill our needs and become our supposed soul mate (however we have defined this). This time, ladies, it's game on!

Back in the day (a phrase one of my best girlfriends uses that always makes me laugh), we sifted through the masses of available horny guys in hopes of meeting a soul mate. We defined our soul mate as the guy who made us feel significant, and we simply couldn't stop thinking about him. He was our male complement; he was perfectly in sync with us and just *got* us. He amplified our strengths and countered our weaknesses. This remarkable man would ask us to marry him, indulge us in a fabulously elaborate wedding and romantic honeymoon, and we would raise beautiful children together and live happily ever after. Doesn't that sound like a fairytale dream come true? For some women, this dream does actualize. However, for many of us, this type of supporting and respectful relationship doesn't ever exist.

Like many women I knew who grew up in the seventies, my mom perpetuated her mother's wish that my partner was responsible for making me happy for the rest of my life. All moms like mine crossed their fingers and prayed that their daughters would be taken care of by a loving man and find joy in marriage. In truth, happiness is no one's responsibility—other than our own. The fundamental nature of finding Mr. Right, getting married, making beautiful babies, and living happily ever after was all too often a set up for much bigger disasters down the road, and no one knew the better.

From infancy, young girls all over the world were, and often still are, taught that marriage is the ultimate goal. Although those exact words may never be spoken out loud, talk of babies and futures with husbands was all it took to solidify the idea that marriage is a necessity. To support this idea further, the media joyfully lines up wedding magazines by the dozen, imposing upon young girls the perfect fairytale dress and the illusion of being whisked away to dream land after the best time of their lives.

Marriage is not the only next step; it is only one option, one choice, one fork in the road of life. Yes, there are always those who conceive it, believe it, and live it, so never underestimate the power of desire and expectation. However, where you are right now as a single forty-plus woman is perfect—even if it doesn't feel so.

For some women who grew up in the sixties and seventies, marriage was the furthest thought in their minds. Instead, a career was the focus. Nonetheless, we were often discouraged from taking this course and led back to the same old story. Sweep us off our feet and let's make babies, please. In my case, making babies was not on my list of priorities. In fact, continuing my education at a college or university did not appeal to me whatsoever after walking school halls for thirteen years. I couldn't imagine anything better than real-life experience to learn how everything worked in the world. My interpretation of success was to get out there, discover, learn from others, and climb the corporate ladder. I can honestly say that my decision to immerse myself in a world driven by Type-A personalities for thirty years taught me more than I could imagine. Whether you can see it or not, the choices you have made throughout your life have supported you.

As someone who is not easily manipulated or confined by rules, working in places where I felt suffocated allowed me to hone my superb people skills. My choices have taken me on a remarkably insightful journey of self-discovery and empowerment. In the end, those old teachings from my mother ensured that I, like many other women of my era, always kept my eyes peeled for Mr. Right, Mr. Perfect, and Mr. Make Me Happy. At the young age of fourteen, I lost my virginity to prove my love for a boy and was soon engaged to be married.

My future was pretty much planned once I agreed to the marriage proposal. My fiancé was to inherit the family farm, and once his grandparents passed, we would move into their home and start building our family. This was certainly not my idea of living a joyful life. At that time though, I couldn't comprehend what I was choosing was my fiancé's definition of a happy life, instead of my own. Due to the early teaching passed down from my mother, I had no idea there were other choices available to me. It seemed I was destined to live a life that far from excited me.

Then, to my surprise, something incredible occurred. During the year my wedding was scheduled, my parents decided to move to another city. I chose to go with them until my big wedding day. This move had its advantages. It wasn't long before young men began to approach me, wanting to "get to know me better!" The realization that getting married was a colossal mistake became quite clear to me. The truth was that I had only agreed to get married because, chances were, I may never be asked again. After all, getting married was what I was supposed to do, right? I had no plans of going to college or university where I would have the opportunity to be introduced to new people. At twenty, we can't grasp the idea of how little life we have lived and how many more exciting adventures there are before us.

Marriage is not the only option, but it was all I could grasp at the time. Getting married appeared to be the next best step. Can you believe I was going to settle? I can. Although your journey may have played out quite differently, did you feel like you settled? Suddenly, I understood that the choices I was making were not in my best interests, and I made the decision to only make choices that made me happy. Soon after this revelation, the next Mr. Right walked into my life. He was young and arrogant, and he made me feel desirable. I enjoyed being seen as a pretty young prize. My eyes were suddenly wide open. I finally understood that my decision to get married was a set up for disaster ... for me!

At this point in the whole divorce/break-up process, you might find yourself thinking, *What now? How did I get here? Why has this happened? This isn't how I imagined my life!* You might even think, *Why did he have to be such a jerk about this whole thing?* The man you wished for and searched for, who was supposed to be with you to the bitter end, till death do us part ... isn't. He is alone like you—or with some chick he left you for. Either way, you're alone.

Some of you (like me) have even secured your sketchy future with children in tow. *Thank goodness for the children. At least I am not totally by myself. I'm not sure I could handle being completely alone.*

I can't tell you how happy I am that my son chose to live with me instead of his father. For me, having to live entirely alone after a twenty-year relationship would be extremely distressing. It's simply too much change and too many feelings of abandonment all at once.

At this point, you may realize that you have no idea who you are anymore. So much of your life has gone by. So many decisions have been made without making your own personal growth part of the picture. You've lived as a we, a couple, or a family for so long that "I" simply doesn't register. I, by myself, with no one to help me, is a fear stirring inside as you do your best to comprehend what it's like to be single again. At night, you look up at your bedroom ceiling and wonder what will happen. How will you do it all alone? What will become of you? Who will help you? Who will love you again?

The feeling that there is no longer any kind of plan can be intimidating.

There is so much to accept when you are forty-plus—and unexpectedly a single woman. The feeling that there is no longer any kind of plan can be intimidating. Does the idea of living the rest of your life alone sadden you? Being single at this age was not what most of us were taught was a normal lifestyle for a woman. So many of us vowed and declared we would never let this happen, saying, "I just can't imagine growing old alone, waiting for someone to come and visit." Yet somehow it has materialized.

In this newfound singledom, the unknown can be most terrifying. Nothing is familiar any longer. Every aspect of your life has been tossed into the air, and you're left wondering where all the pieces are going to land.

Women from my generation were not taught self-love. Okay, maybe some of us were, but I bet they aren't reading this book! We were taught to conform—just as the boys were—except with a different set of rules. So being on your own doesn't feel natural. When you were married, you had a better idea of where you were, even if it was in a bad relationship.

Being married was where you were supposed to be because it was the next step you were taught to take. Now it appears as if there is no direction at all. Do you feel lost in the woods and are trying to find your way home? It's hard to see anything clearly, no matter which direction you look. *Where is the light? How do I get out of here?* Many of you have never been taught how to stand by yourself and trust. Trust is such a magical word—that feeling of closing your eyes and falling, knowing you won't be hurt. You've always had someone there to help you make choices—or make them for you. Now it's simply you, or possibly you, the kids, and their crazy schedules. Maybe your children have grown and don't need your guidance any longer. The feeling of security has all but flown out the window.

For goodness' sake ... you're a single mom!

Chapter Two
WHO'S THAT GIRL IN THE MIRROR?

I remember the first time I was referred to as a single mom. I almost fell off my chair. Literally! The ghastly incident took place on a first date with a man I had met through an Internet dating site. We were happily sipping our lattes and making idle first-date chitchat when he tossed the nasty at me, referring to me as a single mom! Bewildered, I stared at him. After all, being single was new to me. I had been in a relationship for so many years and didn't realize I had morphed into this creature that so many referred to as a single mom.

Those two words conjured up a feast of descriptive words for me to chew on. I suddenly felt at risk of judgment from others. I felt aged, worn, and abandoned like scraps of food no one wanted because they had eaten all the good stuff first. Single mom certainly didn't match the vision I had of myself, but I couldn't deny it. I was, after all, a single woman living with a dependent. However, it still felt all wrong. I wasn't scraps! I knew I had terrific qualities to share.

I went home and considered my definition of a single mom. What was my description of this person I had suddenly become? So many images and emotions flooded my thoughts:

- boring
- a woman who doesn't spend much time on her appearance because she has no one to impress any longer
- tired from having to do everything on her own
- struggling to make ends meet
- miserable
- overwhelmed
- depressed
- poorly dressed (either frumpy or slutty)
- either a man-hater or ready to grab the first guy who comes by and marry him
- insecure
- desperate

Wrong! These descriptions were certainly not how I viewed myself. I had to ask why I had chosen such a definition. Where did it come from? Was it even mine? Was it my mother's definition that I adopted as my own? I tried to recall a single mom in my life who had been an example of these qualities. I'm sure you will agree that the above list doesn't fit you either if you are a single mom. I know many single women raising children who are nothing like this. In fact, they are an inspiration to the courage and strength in women.

I had put on a little weight, but I knew most of it was due to stress and my raging hormones. I had spent years abusing my body through starvation, taking uppers, and experimenting with all sorts of diet programs. It was inevitable that my body would one day reclaim its curvy exterior and tell me to go to hell. Does this sound familiar? How my body looks now isn't something I am settling with, but I do respect the way I look as the way I look right now. I know everything is temporary. I had to wonder how much of that weight is emotional. Are the extra pounds actually you waiting for happiness in your life instead of making it yourself? Is the way you look now is exactly how you expected to look at this age?

I came to the conclusion that if I met a man who didn't like my curves, he could get lost. I have always paid attention to the way I look. I love putting on make-up, styling my hair, and dressing in ways that compliment my figure. I feel insecure and overwhelmed most days, due to my work environment and current single situation, but I do my best to ensure this isn't common knowledge. When I walk, I walk with confidence, or so I've been told. I have never appeared to be a woman with low self-esteem, even though there have been times throughout my life where I have experienced self-love anorexia. I have always believed that a woman who loves herself and is confident is sexy. She walks differently, and people take notice. So I did my best to be that which I wanted to be. Why not fake it till you make it.

Ask yourself where you fit in? Have you ever thought about it? Do you even care? In the blink of an eye, you went from being single, to being married, and then back to single again. Only this time, being single is a whole different slice of pie. Perhaps you are a single mom and feel utterly out of place due to some wonky definition. Goodness knows you've learned a lot since you were last single. You've most likely lived through a ton of heartache and drama. Some of you have achieved considerable success in your careers, and others have raised families. Your friends may all be married, which may make you feel as though you are the third wheel at social gatherings.

What's fantastic is that you have a much clearer picture of what you want in a relationship. You have the perfect example of what didn't work for you. Most of the single men you have to choose from are all in the same place you are now—only on the opposite side and paying their exes every month. This is the time to be proud of who and where you are in your life. Why shouldn't you be?

The problem with most women who have lived through separation or divorce or are in the middle of such a life-altering event is that they feel betrayed, shunned, dumped, hated, or taken advantage of. They're throwing themselves a pity party or a man-hater party instead of celebrating all they have achieved. Living through the break-up is proof that you can handle just about anything. The marriage was a substantial contribution and learning experience. It is scary to be alone after feeling that you had so much security. I know this all too well. But this is your chance to actually be you—and to rediscover yourself again.

Part of the rediscovery process is figuring out what you think about the person looking back at you in the mirror.

Go ahead and take a look in the mirror. Would you want to be with her? Does she look fun? Is there a spark in her eyes—or are they tired and lifeless? Have you ever taken a good look? I remember the first time I walked by a mirror and didn't recognize who was looking back at me. I had put on a few pounds, but that wasn't it. I had aged, but that wasn't it either. It was the story my eyes told that threw me off. They could have been anyone's eyes, but not mine! There was no sparkle, passion, or excitement in those eyes.

My mother once said, "There comes a time in your life when you look in the mirror and don't recognize who you see looking back at you. You have a picture of who you are and what you look like in your mind—and the two just don't match."

At the time I assumed she meant age, and maybe she did. However, I believe it's much deeper than what we see on the surface.

That day I looked into my eyes in the full-length mirror, an odd sense of detachment washed over me. Have you ever felt this way? How many times had I checked out my butt, admired myself in a new pair of heels, primped my hair and makeup, or scowled at a new zit popping up on my chin in that mirror before heading out the door? It was always me looking back, only in an older body. So when my eyes told a different story, I was quite frazzled.

It can be somewhat unnerving to stare deeply into your own eyes. However, doing so gives you a good idea of your relationship with *you*. On that day, there was remarkably little connection or electricity in those eyes looking back at me. I was rather creeped out by the whole experience, to tell the truth. The day the stranger appeared in the mirror occurred sometime in the last three years of my marriage. I had become quite proficient at swallowing my pain, and it was about to burst out through my eyes! They weren't simply lifeless; they were in pain. I hadn't realized how sad my whole face appeared.

Most of us are under the impression that we can hide how we feel from the outside world, but people take notice far more than you know. There are people watchers out there, like me, who are watching and analyzing, simply for the thrill of it.

About a week after the stranger revealed herself in the mirror, I was standing in line to order my morning latte when a devilishly handsome man turned and faced me in line. He said, "You would be so much prettier if you smiled."

Can you believe this? I was so shocked by this total stranger's comment that I couldn't respond. Who would say such a thing to a stranger? Oh yes. People like me!

If you are a single mom at this point in your life, what kind of single mom are you? If you are not a single mom, what is the definition you give to yourself? Being honest isn't always easy, but it feels fantastic when you allow your truth to shine from within. Once you begin to get real with yourself, you can start to bypass some of the crap you've bought into. You can start redefining and reconstructing who you genuinely are. This saves having a stranger point it out to you! So take a look. What do your eyes tell you when you look in the mirror? Who's in there? What does she think about most often? Get up close and personal with those eyes. Lean right in and take a long, deep look.

The first time I did this exercise, I had to turn away. I was experiencing a horrible day where nothing was going well at work, and I took one of my famous breaks in the washroom. Whenever I was experiencing major difficulties at work, I escaped and hid behind a closed door. After hanging out there for a while, questioning how I was going to free myself of this place, I walked up to the mirror, looked myself right in the eyes, and said, "I love you."

Anger immediately welled up inside me. Instead of responding with love, I pointed an accusing finger at that person in the mirror and said, "Liar!"

In that moment, I felt only disgust toward myself. I was ashamed at what I had allowed myself to become—for not being true to who I am, for keeping myself small, and for believing others could control me. Tears streamed down my cheeks, and I became acutely aware of how much I had been fooling myself by spending so much energy pretending to fit into a life I didn't agree with.

Give it a try yourself. It will be unnerving at first, but see if you can get a peek at who is actually in there. What vibe do you get when you stare into your eyes? Do you feel the need to turn away? Do your eyes appear sad, lifeless, overwhelmed, tired, puffy from crying, angry, restless, unworthy, lonely, damaged, or fearful? I'm sure you've heard that the eyes are the window or mirror to the soul. Your eyes are a reflection of who you are. We collect experiences in our brains through our eyes. Fear, sadness, loneliness, and happiness are all revealed through the eyes. Models are asked to pose and let their eyes convey a particular emotion for the camera to capture.

Don't be upset if your eyes tell a story you would rather they didn't, as mine did. Simply be thankful you have begun to identify some of the pain you've been attempting to cover up. From this new realization, you can set off learning how to use tools of distraction, the power of positive thinking, self-love techniques, journal-writing exercises, or perhaps a life coach to guide you in a more loving direction. The important factor is that you have reached out to yourself and made a connection.

What if you could look into your own eyes and discover joy and empowerment?

Many of us live our lives as if we are one of the walking dead. We follow the masses and keep ourselves ordinary. We don't break any rules; we stay in the background and keep ourselves small and unnoticeable. What if your life could be fun and exciting? What if you could turn this whole situation around and use this experience as a springboard to a new life? What if you could look into your eyes and discover joy and empowerment?

Pushing Your Own Buttons

Once you've played with this first step, and caught your eyes in the act of hiding your pain, you can go one step further and use your mirror image to uncover even more of your inner turmoil. This exercise is a little tricky at first, but is extremely beneficial once you get the hang of it.

This exercise involves talking to yourself in the mirror. Stand in front of a mirror, a good arm's length away. Imagine the mirror version of you is the all-knowing you, your inner goddess, or your higher self. This exercise can also be done by placing two chairs across from each other, and moving back and forth between them, playing different roles—you and the all-knowing you.

The all-knowing you asks questions that push your emotional buttons. You shift mentally back and forth between the real you and the all-knowing you. The all-knowing you can see all of your little tricks. After all, she is the broader version of who you really are. She knows when you are lying. She can read between your lines. She knows what your truth is, and she will not stand for anything less than honesty from you. This exercise involves a desire to connect with you—and an understanding that everything you have ever desired to know comes from within.

Here are some sample questions to get you started. Choose the ones that work best for you:

- Who are you?
- What is it you really want right now?
- Why do you continue to complain about your situation all the time?
- Why are you pretending to be emotionally strong when you are really torn apart inside?
- Why do you feel like you are a victim in this situation?
- What advantage does being a victim give you?
- What would make you happy right now?
- What do you love about you?

- How do you feel today?
- Why do you feel this way?
- What's pissing you off the most lately?
- What are you jealous about?
- Why do you think bad stuff always happens to you?
- Why do you feel as though everything is out of your control?
- Why do you feel like a failure?
- What are you covering up?
- Why do you feel like you can't ask for help?
- Why do you think you have to do everything on your own?
- What are you afraid of?
- What would you do if you weren't afraid?
- How many people have you talked to this week about how crappy your situation is?

As you play this back-and-forth game, allow your emotions to come out. Yell at yourself if you feel the need. Be honest when answering the all-knowing you. Cry if you need to. Sleep if that is what your body calls for after this exercise. Go out with a friend if need be. The key is to make a connection with your inner electrifying being—and feel the love she has for you. In the beginning, it may feel as if she is mean and nasty, but she is all about love. Create a link to her, and you can stop begging outside sources to save you. Plug back into your electricity and power as a single woman.

Try this exercise for five days. Keep a record of what you unearth during these conversations. If the mirror version is too intimidating, try the chair option. Becoming aware of your truths is magical. Connecting with your emotions, thoughts, and the labels you have given to yourself is the first step toward rediscovering who you are. The unknown, after all, can appear to be much more fearful.

You are, in fact, a beautiful person who has simply forgotten how magnetic and electrifying you are. Imagine how wonderful your life is becoming as you expose limiting beliefs and stuck points and step into ease and joy.

Chapter Three
WHEN FEAR BECOMES A FACTOR

Now that I am single, I'm surprised at how many forty-plus women are also single. Isn't it fascinating how when you are married, everyone around you appears to also be married—and when you are single, everyone else is single? I'm forty-eight and can't believe how many women my age—and older—are living without a partner. I always assumed at this point in my life I would be off traveling the world with my husband and running several businesses. I have pictured my life that way for as long as I can remember.

I'm sure most of you had some sort of plan designed for your future as well. After all, we are all taught to set long-term goals that match what society dictates as being acceptable. These can be more setups for disaster. "What's your five- and ten-year plan?" This question is asked by parents, teachers, mentors, business advisors, and bosses. Unfortunately, long-term goals lock us in and often set us up for failure.

Because long-term goals are set in the distant future, we don't put our efforts now into making them a reality. Plus, when we do reach that looming date of supposed manifestation, we feel like crap if we don't see our dream or goal materializing. If you set a long-term goal at age fifteen to be married by age thirty, but you don't achieve it, how do you feel? If you set a long-term goal to have a specific amount of money in your savings account by age forty, and you don't achieve it, how do you feel? Like a failure, right? When we don't meet these long-term goals, we believe we have crossed some magical point of no return. We've wasted all this time and failed!

I'd like to introduce you to the idea of engaging in short-term quests instead of long-term goals. Quests are so much more enjoyable. On a quest, we have one objective to focus our efforts toward. Goals are set way out there in the future, beyond our grasp. Quests are happening now. They are like mini goals that allow you to concentrate on one thing at a time, now, and they are easier to refine because you see results much sooner. If you aren't getting the outcome you desire, try going at it from a different angle.

I certainly didn't think I would be starting my life all over again at forty-eight. Does this mean I'm a failure because I screwed up my long-term goal? Definitely not! What if everything I have always desired simply shows up in a totally different way than I originally expected? When you don't understand how powerful playing with quests can be in crafting your life—versus setting long-term goals—it's easy to let fear creep in.

It's no wonder specific fears seem more common with us single newbs. Not that married women are fearless or anything. When you are single at this age, after being in a long relationship, your fears are quite different from those of married women. Plus, being single at this point in a woman's life is a great deal different than being single in your twenties.

Perhaps you have the fear of not being able to provide for yourself or your children. I recently quit my job as a creative manager. It's the kind of job everyone thinks of as being fun. Being creative is fun, but making ads, signs, catalogs, and brochures within tight deadlines is stressful. The design industry is rapidly changing with the growth of the Internet, and many designers my age are struggling to stay in the game. Being unemployed, I can say this fear is at the top of my mind.

Many of us also fear not having the backup income of a mate or having someone who supports us. We may not believe anyone has our back—or that we have a go-to person to help us through difficult situations. We can seek advice and support from our friends, but friends offer vastly different help and advice than a *loving* partner does. We may also fear growing old alone, getting sick without anyone to look after us, questioning our retirement plan, or jumping back into the dating scene.

I once overheard a single woman and a married woman talking. The single woman was explaining how she had heard that having neck adjustments from a chiropractor could have disastrous results. She was concerned, and had decided to cease any further neck adjustments immediately, even though the treatments were providing her relief from an old injury.

The married woman was dumbfounded. She said, "What could be wrong with having your neck adjusted? Having your neck adjusted keeps your spine in alignment so you don't have pain and headaches."

Her words fell on fearful, newly separated single mom ears and were quickly counteracted. The single mom had heard that a neck adjustment could result in a splintering of bones, which could lead to death!

The married woman could not contain herself and broke out laughing. "Surely you have to be kidding! You can't live in fear of such a thing happening."

The single mom became terribly upset at what appeared to be a lack of concern the married women had regarding her health, and defending her decision, she exclaimed, "I'm a single mom now! I have two children to look after. It's very important that I can be there for them! After all, I'm all they have now that I am on my own!"

The married woman was not impressed. After all, her children were just as valuable to her—with or without her husband. Being married didn't make her any less relevant to her children. She was quite insulted at the single woman's comments and the conversation soon ended.

This is a perfect example of how a single, newly separated, forty-plus mom could feel that she has no one to count on or turn to. Many women in this situation live in fear of what could happen next and conjure up all sorts of horrible possibilities. It's certainly more on the minds of single moms than it is for women who are married. The negative what-if syndrome easily sneaks in and consumes their thoughts. After all, they have just turned their lives upside down, and they are usually in an empty, negative space that is totally alien to them.

Being in the same situation, I sometimes find it a struggle not to engage fear. Something will happen that spirals me into a roller-coaster fear ride, flipping my stomach upside down and twisting it into knots. A good hour or so of crying and feeling severely depressed usually follows, making me all the more aware of how alone I am.

For years, you were married or sharing your life with a partner. You felt pretty secure. You had some stuff—a house, a car, a pond in your backyard with lawn chairs and bug zappers. You were on the road to an easier life where you and your spouse would retire to do whatever caught your fancy—or so you had hoped. Now, you are staring at the darn bedroom ceiling alone every night. You've replayed the past ten years, or more, trying to figure out where you went wrong. Blaming you. Blaming him. Blaming. Blaming. Blaming. Some of you have even bored your friends, family, coworkers, and hairdressers to tears with your woes.

If you find the main topic of your conversations these days includes how awful he is being, how crappy what he did to you was, or how tough he is making everything for you, you're boring your friends to tears. You need to change that story and move on to better topics. Believe me, it will help you so much more than you can see right now.

Every time you tell that story, you reactivate the negative emotions/vibes as a whole new experience in your body.

Each time you recall a past experience in your mind, you choose only specific pieces of the actual event to connect with. Then, you break it down even further, only feeling what you remember at that time, perhaps due to a dispute that may have occurred right before your marriage ended, an argument that took place over a year ago, or even how horrible you felt every night you waited for him to come home.

The mind functions on perception. Each time you relive an old memory, you perceive it differently than when it happened the first time, due to your current circumstances. In doing so, you experience different emotions surrounding the entire memory, again, depending on your current situation. This creates a new emotional experience in your body. Wow! It is as if the battle has never ended. You keep creating new, nasty, emotional experiences in your body based on the emotions most prominent around the old memory, over and over and over again. But there is good news. As deeply as you ache now over all of the pain from your separation, that is how deeply you will feel loved when you resolve some of these old battle wounds.

If every time you spend time with a friend, you persistently talk about your ex and the rotten stuff you experienced, or are still going through regarding the breakup, you may as well be *barfing* on them! Barfing is a term I use to refer to negative conversations where you continually repeat an old story without the intention of finding a solution. Why barfing? Think about it. Barf stinks! It's a smell you simply can't get rid of. Even when you change your clothes, you swear you can still smell it. It's pretty nasty stuff. This is what you are projecting onto the poor people you call your friends, and you continue to regurgitate your negativity onto them. Your friends leave conversations feeling uncomfortable and later spend time worrying about you. This is not good. They have experienced some of your pain and have associated it with a past experience of their own. What does this do? It creates a negative experience in their bodies, surrounding something they may not have thought about for ages.

We all relate someone else's pain to our own personal experiences or fears. I'm sure the definition of friendship does not include making me feel your pain every time we speak until I feel as terrible as you do so we can sit on the floor crying together and not solve anything. Seriously? This is a far cry from being a shoulder to cry on, wouldn't you agree? The barf you are so freely spreading around isn't beneficial to anyone. It also proves you are not looking for a resolution to grant yourself any relief. Your friends may have some pretty impressive things going on in their lives that they feel they can't share with you because they worry their good news may hurt your feelings. What purpose does this all serve you?

When it comes to your definition of a friend, being a loyal dumping ground for someone's fears and gloom is not a supportive definition. How would you define a friend? Think about it. When you define a friend as being someone you can go to when you need help, do you mean at any time of day? How much do you actually expect from them? Many also define a friend as someone who can keep a secret. Is it actually fair to expect others to be the bearers of our deep, dark secrets? When we say a friend is a shoulder to cry on, how long does that imply?

There are always times when we need to vent and have someone listen to our woes, but how long should we expect our friends to remain silent? In fact, listening without interjecting is relatively difficult for most of us. I believe that what most of us are looking for in a friend is the sense that they *get* us. We want to be seen for who we are and feel we can be ourselves around these special people in our lives.

It makes me wonder about the stresses of society today—and how we project them onto each other. No one can form a friendship or relationship until both parties realize that being friends is not about meeting each other's needs. This would be an exceptionally conditional relationship. Your friends love you, but they should not be responsible for meeting your needs. We are all here to experience joy as radiant beings. I believe those we surround ourselves with are a direct reflection of who we are.

Anaïs Nin summed it up beautifully when she said, "Each friend represents a world in us, and a world not born until they arrive, and it is only by this meeting that a new world is born."

We do indeed have unique relationships with each and every person we connect with. Perhaps one of your friends is an expert at making you feel better, and another may inspire you to be all you can be. Why would we choose to continually barf negative self-talk all over our friends?

Friendships have become much more complicated and now include a tag-team variety of interactions using social media. Most would agree a close friend is someone we have met in person and choose to invest our trust in. We believe they have our best interests in mind. They are extraordinary individuals who share in our lives and challenge us to be our best selves.

These unique individuals we choose to connect with tend to be people we interact with and see frequently, and they generally fit into the same social group as we do. For example, single moms typically have other single mom friends who share common interests. This offers a common bond and allows us to support each other.

Some would say friendship is akin to companionship. Friends have our backs during emotional crises (Translation: someone I can regularly dump my emotions on who will sit quietly and listen). This is where it all goes wrong. Yes, friends are there for us, and most have soggy shoulders from sopping up our woes, but they are also there to kick us in the butt when we need it.

A friend is someone I connect with, hang out with from time to time, and who has a positive impact on my life, as I do in some way on theirs. Our hidden agendas—and the desire to be seen—cause us to construct a massive list of expectations for our friends to live up to. These same expectations often leave us feeling disgruntled when we do not receive from our friends in the same ways we give of ourselves. We unconsciously twist "treat others as you wish to be treated" into "I expect you to treat me according to my list of friend expectations." The result is that we do not adore and appreciate our friends for all they are and have to offer to the personal expansion and empowerment of our lives.

Children actually have better relationships with their friends than most adults do. Most kids make friends easily because they spend more time playing than working with their peers. When selecting friends, children subconsciously go through a detailed checklist. The primary question is whether this person is going to be fun to play with. They will often approach each other and say, "Hey, do you want to be my friend?" Of course, this is not the case with all children, but it is for the vast majority. However, that is when big people like to poke our noses into their interactions and show them how it's done.

The best way to teach our children how to build strong friendships is to be a shining example. If you are constantly whining and complaining to your friends, or about them, imagine what your kids will do with theirs?

Perhaps the next time you talk to a friend, coworker, or family member, even if they bring up the subject of your separation/ divorce before you do, you could do everyone a favor and change the subject.

Some would choose to see this as a form of denial. I'm not asking you to lie or pretend everything is peachy when this is not how you feel. Instead, you could share that you are still working through some things, but you are developing a clearer picture of what you want. The road to redefining you is not formed through sharing and reliving your fears and painful experiences, especially with those you love. We've already discussed the effects this has on the body. Now that you have blinked and chosen a new fork in your road, it's time to start exposing some of these fears and move forward. It's the only way to go after all—even if you don't believe it.

What's Your Story?

I have found that the best way to flip the switch is to let go of that old story you keep repeating to everyone. How about letting go of it verbally? What if you stopped saying that crappy story out loud and told a different story?

Imagine what it would feel like to talk about how you desire your life to be instead of how rotten you perceive it as being right now. Is it possible for you to share how enjoyable it is to be in charge of your own experiences, stating how marvelous you feel about being able to make your own choices and not having to check in with anyone? How much pleasure would there be in creating a new story? Delight in sprinkling it with a buzz of excitement regarding how empowering it is to be able to do what you want, when you want, and how you want. Share what you love about your life *right now*. Are you enjoying eating foods your ex turned his nose up at? When you sleep, do you enjoy having the whole bed to yourself? Maybe you even choose to leave it unmade in the morning? How perfect is it for you to be able to spend time with yourself? Do you have any idea how many married women crave a few hours alone? Find anything you can in your life that is working right now—and put a spotlight on it.

I fully understand fear. I was in a long relationship and am now reconstructing my life. I now pay all the bills on my own, take care of my son, am rebuilding my life coach business that I let go in the turmoil, and building a TeleWebSeries business, all while hoping I can take care of myself. Sometimes I worry that if I make one little mistake, everything will crash down on me. These thoughts mentally send us spiraling. I find the key to keeping this particular fear at bay is to find ways to distract myself from it. When I can distract myself, I detach from the fear and start the process of wiping out old patterns and beliefs about what I think my life is supposed to look like. As soon as you start thinking about how fearful you are that something will happen, you need to create a distraction.

Fear is simply a pattern you've created in your mind due to repeating similar experiences. Like many women, you may not have ever been exclusively by yourself for very long, and you conjure up all sorts of scary scenarios in this new, unknown single territory. After all, the unknown is keeping so many of us from moving forward, and I'm speaking from experience here. But I promise that it's all just a head game ... created by you, for you.

Many women have stories about how they were taken advantage of. You may even have examples of what happened to a friend whose husband took everything while she was at work, a neighbor whose ex emptied her bank account, or a cousin who came home to a letter telling her he was through with the marriage, leaving everything for her to figure out on her own. For some of you, one of these circumstances is your personal experience! But to be frank—what happened to any of these other people is not *your* experience. Even if it feels similar, it is not your experience.

The desire to be in charge of your life and begin living from right where you are, right now, is essential. Let the past be in the past. Build on what you have in this moment, while engaging your passions. I'd like to share my morning shower chant with you.

"Today I will only pay attention to what brings me joy. I release myself from all limitations I am holding on to now. Today I will only give my attention to joyful things."

These words have helped me start each day with a positive focus. Joy cannot be found in your present environment if you are talking about all the people, places, circumstances, and events you have decided were wrong. Joy and misery simply cannot coexist in the same space. If you desire joy, then choose to fuel your heart with the idea that there are endless possibilities in front of you.

I know all this love stuff sounds like hoopla, but do you ever notice when you expect the worst to happen, it usually does? I choose to believe that this whole idea of reality is crap, at least in the sense that there are only limited ways that events can play out. We get so caught up in the details and specifics of what we can only *imagine* being possible that we forget there may be a million other possibilities for how something could unfold.

In my opinion, there is no such thing as reality. Reality is built out of our own personal experiences, which are viewpoints and perceptions we have decided upon, about an environment or experience we are living at any given moment. I could stand directly beside you, having lived entirely different life experiences, look at exactly the same scene, and see it from an altogether different perspective. What you may view as lack, I may consider a possibility. What you consider being destructive, I may appreciate as a new beginning. What you view as reality is only for you.

As a life coach, I encourage people to see themselves as the center of their own universe. I know this way of viewing ourselves goes against everything most of us have been taught. However, when you look at the world as revolving around you, you can appreciate that your health and happiness are essential in order for you to help those in your life. Without you, so many lives would change—or cease to be! Your influence on others would never have happened. That's why listening to all the nasty experiences that have happened to others, and worrying they may happen in the same way to you, is so destructive. Their experiences are uniquely their own, and they would not play out in exactly the same way for you. What appears real to you right now is only temporary. With every new choice you make, you change where you are. Just because something happened in a specific way to fifty other people, or some statistic or study says something happens to one in every five people, it is not proof it will unfold in that precise way for you.

Fear is simply a pattern you have bought into, so why not break the pattern? You will not break the pattern by saying, "But, but, but." It is most beneficial to find ways to distract you from your fears, as I mentioned earlier. Some of you may be experiencing some pretty scary stuff. If so, you need to seek professional assistance to learn about your rights. Please don't hesitate to do so. There are a number of free places to go that offer women assistance in such matters. Many of us are taken advantage of simply because we don't know our rights.

The next things to figure out are what you are fearful of and how you can distract yourself. Since I have no idea who you are, I'm going to share some of my fears and how they can be converted into more positive outcomes. I hope some will feel familiar to you.

The Fear of Losing My Job

I did everything in my power to hold on to a job I knew was killing me. I worked in an environment where, from my perspective, people did not love or respect each other ... at least not upper management. This was extremely toxic for me. I was also progressing spiritually and rediscovering myself, which added to my frustration. The more I became aware that I was, indeed, the creator of my life experiences, the more I was motivated to find ways to distract myself from constantly worrying about my current circumstance.

How did I distract myself? I know this is going to make you laugh, but when I left work, *I cut my butt-cords.* Yes, I said butt-cords! I became aware that I was allowing myself to stay plugged into a negative, draining environment—hours after I left it. You know exactly what I mean, don't you? You go home and share the events of your day to whoever is available to listen. Or worse, you continue to replay the day's events in your mind, creating new responses (that was my favorite). Perhaps you toy with new scenarios for how it could have played out differently—if only you would have had the guts to stand up for yourself. You just don't leave it alone! I knew this nasty environment was bogging up my rational thinking, so as I walked out the door at the end of the day, I would swipe my hand across my butt and envision unplugging from that toxic energy. This exercise helps you detach from a previous environment or situation you have twisted your thoughts around.

The next step is to open your senses to everything in front of you. Smell the fresh air whether the season is spring, summer, winter, or fall. Open your eyes to the world around you. Actually see what's been in front of you, hundreds of times before, that you never paid attention to. Once I swipe my hand across my butt, I tell myself to release that old situation and embrace this new one.

This exercise may sound silly, but it cuts the mental cord holding me to fear and disempowerment, and it brings my focus to the present moment. Fear is in the mind, and it is in the mind that I set myself free. I know there are at least six waking hours in front of me where I am in a completely different place, and I open myself fully to this instead. What most of us do is jump in our cars, crank up the radio, and push our way home through traffic. What if you could create a peaceful ride home? What if you actually looked at the world around you as you were driving and took in some of the amazing scenery? What if you took a different route home? The secret is in the mental unplugging.

I don't care if anyone is watching or worry about what they may think if they happen to see me swiping my hand across my behind. I think, *That's done. Now this here surrounding me, what my eyes are seeing in this moment, is what is important for me to focus on to feel happy.*

I suggest starting this process of releasing fears every chance you get. These things that have always been there, without you having paid attention to them, need your attention—now!

The Fear of Not Having Enough Money

This one certainly hit home with me, especially since I no longer have a job! A lot of women get a pretty sweet deal when they break up their marriage, but there are many of us who don't. So what's this fear all about? Lack. In the midst of letting go of a marriage or a relationship, we have shifted into lack. And here is the secret hidden gem! What we are genuinely fearful of is that we believe we have failed; we have a core belief that there is a painful consequence connected to failure.

Part of the fear of not having enough money is also built from the comfort zone we have created for ourselves. We fear what we will lose, which when looked at further, is connected to the fear of judgment. So how can you distract yourself from all of this? By unplugging from those beliefs and consciously shifting out of lack and into abundance.

It seems now more than ever that we have a difficult time separating life and money. We associate "having money" and "wealth" with abundance. The distracter in this situation is to shift into feelings of abundance. I'm referring to the feeling rather than a dollar amount. Appreciation is a state of abundance. What do you have that money simply cannot buy? Start appreciating all that is fulfilling and amazing in your life today. Get your journal out and make a list of everything in your life that is gratifying, refreshing, and satisfying. Start by simply looking around at your surroundings and making note of any items you love. What time of year is it? Is there an event or holiday coming up that you may be looking forward to? Are you in fact loving this gift of time that you have given yourself to focus on rediscovering you and your passions? What do you love doing? Perhaps you enjoy baking, looking up new recipes, planting flowers, walking your dog, scrapbooking, visiting friends, soaking up some sun, or even going to work. Simply focus your attention on anything you can appreciate and make a list.

The Fear of Intimacy and Dating

Because so many of us are afraid of being hurt again, we avoid becoming emotionally committed or attached. If we do find ourselves in a relationship, we often sabotage it unknowingly.

In the beginning of relationships, when people are feeling fabulous, they often call up sabotaging thoughts from past experiences:

- What if he gets tired of me?
- How come he hasn't talked about us living together? Maybe he's not that into me.
- We spend a lot of time together; maybe he's too clingy and is looking for someone to take care of him.
- I wonder how long it will be before he starts to show his true colors, and I won't like who he really is?

These sabotaging thoughts, drawn on from past experiences, instantly put limitations on new relationships, and they start to turn you off. Think about every instance where you have started a love relationship—and begun to doubt it. That's you sabotaging the relationship. Most of us have forgotten what it is like to date and are reluctant to connect emotionally. We are drowning in the fear of disapproval and rejection. The dating scene feels so unfamiliar, and we have all but forgotten how to flirt or show affection. We are afraid to fall in love again or show a desire for physical closeness. Closing off from these emotions is not a good idea.

After months on my own, I decided to look into what online dating sites were all about. I was surprised by how many people over forty are single! I began to wonder how other women identified themselves in this online environment and decided to play with running searches from a man's perspective to see what would show up. Wow! There are a lot of us! I was surprised to see how different our expectations are at this seasoned age compared to younger people searching online for a mate.

I would suggest finding a free site and checking it out just for fun. I'm not saying to put yourself out there if you are not ready to. Just read what some of the men write about themselves, to get an idea about their needs. You will see everything from sports fanatics to couch potatoes. The more of these portfolios I read, the more I saw most men's stories said, "This is the way I am, this is my job, these are my likes, and this is what I enjoy doing," or "I need a woman to complete me." The men, in fact, don't have any better idea regarding what they want in a mate than we do! Like us, they only know what they are familiar with (what went wrong in their last relationships).

Have fun filling in the questionnaires and seeing what comes up for you. It's a fun distraction exercise. Simply toy with the idea of dating. Why not give it a try?

The Fear of Being Alone

Is this a familiar fear for you? The last time I was on my own, I was twenty-three. From that age forward, I was with the same partner.

Being single again is a rather freaky feeling, although at the same time, I quite enjoy it.

When the fear of being alone creeps in, many women try to appease it by going on the hunt for a man. Being on our own doesn't feel natural to many of us. We aren't sure how to be with ourselves, and many of us may not be sure we even like who we are.

What's so incredible about being with yourself now is that you get to do things you want to do. Ladies, it's time for another distraction. A good distraction will stop you from focusing your thoughts on being alone. It's something that makes you feel as though you are the luckiest lady alive. There are married women all over the world who would die for some time to themselves. They would adore some quiet time to read or watch whatever they choose on television—or never to have to sit through another hockey or soccer game.

What do *you* want to do? What activities would be good distractions for you? What types of interests have you kept secret? What have you always secretly desired to do, that if pursued in your last relationship, you may have been accused of being immature or a bit crazy? Think beyond what is considered normal by everyone else. I have always been a curious type; if something interested to me, I explored it. I have explored many unusual interests. I'll name a few and maybe one will pique your interest.

Energy Healing Methods

No matter who I spoke to, I kept hearing about a new healing method. Just for fun, I chose to check some of them out.

I was first led to a hands-on energy healing technique called Reiki. I was surprised by how something so simple could produce such impressive results, and I immersed myself in Reiki classes until I become a Reiki Master Teacher Practitioner. This led me to seek out other healing modalities where I continued my exploration in Blue Matrix Energy Healing, Integrated Energy Therapy, dowsing, chakra balancing, six sensory development, Hooponopono, and Access Consciousness. Traditional healing methods had never appealed to me. I always felt conventional remedies never got to the root of our real emotional issues, but playing with these New Age methods opened my eyes to what was possible in the world of healing. They also provided me with a new circle of friends—something that is tremendously beneficial during alone time.

A New Way of Thinking

The teachings of the Law of Attraction have introduced me to a most powerful, life-altering exploration of self and provided me with a whole new perspective on life. After years of using these techniques and processes to find joy, *The Secret* movie was introduced to the masses. People everywhere jumped on the Law of Attraction train— and then off again. Although this new way of thinking appeared straightforward at first, many couldn't embrace the concepts full time. I, of course, never jumped off. This would be the thing that is your best-kept secret. The concept you would have liked to learn more about—but were afraid of how you would be judged.

It might be a good idea to go to your favorite bookstore. Don't go online; actually get your butt over to a store and walk around. Grab your favorite beverage and peruse the store to see what topics catch your eye. Get over to the Self-Help and New Age sections where all the weird stuff is—and check it out.

A New Creative Urge

One day, I decided to try my hand at painting. I went to the craft store for supplies to fill this new creative urge. Not knowing what exactly to paint, I simply began filling the canvas. Time passed without me even realizing it, and those old fearful thoughts were nowhere in sight. Painting, so it seemed, was the perfect distraction. Now, whenever I am frustrated or lonely, I paint. Perhaps instead of painting, you love photography, writing, or cooking? Whatever! Search for something you enjoy doing that fills up some of the time you are using to worry.

Connect with Your Body

Connecting with your body is a fantastic distracter, and there are tons of ways to play. You could take up yoga, martial arts, tai chi, belly-dancing, or jogging. Anything that gets you out of your head and paying attention to your body is beneficial. I personally enjoy meditation. Some find meditation difficult, but if it sounds like something you've always wanted to try, I suggest Summer McStravick's *Flow Dreaming* or finding some good guided meditations to listen to. My favorite meditations are from Colette Baron-Reid, a Canadian intuitive counselor.

No matter what your situation, it's critical to know that you are the most prominent person in your life. You can choose to live feeling scared and miserable—or you can be happy. You aren't alone; you are simply doing your own thing right now. Sign up for a class of some sort, something artsy to engage the creative right side of your brain. Get to the gym and give your body some attention. Start walking or go to the bookstore and choose something to read you would never have chosen before ... just for the change. Distract yourself from the fear of being alone.

You must find a distraction! Using distraction as a tool doesn't mean you are burying your head in the sand or hiding from some truth everyone else calls reality. There is that word again ... reality! It drives me crazy every time I hear it. Why? Because the people who use the word reality are usually saying, "Face the facts. Stop feeling sorry for yourself and get back to your life the way it was before."

They are asking you to go back to what they define as normal. Your life certainly wasn't working for you; what's to get back to?

Did you know that every time you knowingly seek out something uplifting to make you feel good, you shift out of pain and suffering? So use that! Go rent all the comedy movies you can and laugh, laugh, laugh. This will get those endorphins rushing through your body. Break up the fear in your chest that makes you feel as though you can't breathe. Better yet, do some deep breathing exercises. When you are fearful, you breathe in short breaths. This is not good for your body; it needs oxygen. The best distraction to use when you begin to think fearful thoughts is to take five long, deep breaths. Deep breathing changes the patterns in your body. I use this technique all the time. Give it a try.

These are just a few of the fears that many new single women are tackling. I hope I have provided you with some encouragement to begin your own healing process using distraction. Start living your life in ways you desire it to be lived—and not how you see it with your eyes or trying to remember how it was.

Pretend, pretend, and pretend some more. Get silly. Stop looking for proof to support misery. Appeal to the child in you to come out and play. Goodness knows she is tired of sitting on the sidelines while you play grown-up. Consciously change those fearful thought patterns. Feel the spark of hope and love for self as it starts flowing through your body.

Chapter Four
EMBRACING SINGLE JUST A LITTLE

The bedroom ceiling is still staring at you when you wake up every morning, and at night, it's just you. My dog, Chester Pug, shares my bed, and I must say I'm exceedingly happy to have him. Although, he does take over—and sheds like no dog I have ever had the opportunity to live with—I enjoy having him and don't feel so alone. Goodness! That little dog knows exactly how to position himself around my body, making me contort into the most uncomfortable sleeping positions! I have to wonder if this skill is basic training for all dogs and cats before they are adopted by humans since all other animal owners who allow their pets to sleep with them seem to share this common complaint. However, it's not all that different from being woken up several times through the night because of someone snoring inches from your head. That is something I don't miss. I would prefer waking up to a loving, smiling human who loves me to pieces! For now, it's Chester Pug and me. He gives the best morning snuggles and kisses ever! He is also a terrific listener and tolerates my woes while I lavish him with attention. My life dramas don't seem to bother him in the least.

Nevertheless, let's be women and look at this whole single situation as women usually do … emotionally. Yes, even those of you who let your tough, left, masculine brain call the shots need to play along and pay attention to your gut feelings for a moment. From right where you are, stand up and say out loud, "I'm single."

I'm serious, ladies. Don't say it in your head; say it out loud. You've got a voice; let it be heard. When you hear yourself say something out loud, you claim it. This is why we often don't actually speak our dreams and desires—because when we do, we then feel the need to act on them.

Once you say those words loudly and clearly, the next step is to describe how saying and hearing them made you feel. This is all about emotion. That's right; no more shutting them down and ignoring them! If you're not sure how or what you felt, say it again. I want you to say those words out loud until you feel something stir somewhere in your body. Why? Your body responds by releasing a light feeling you may interpret as a fluttering in your chest or stomach, or as something heavy like nervousness, anxiety, emptiness, or nausea. Whatever the feeling is, it's essential to note where you felt it in your body, and whether or not it felt empowering (light) or disempowering (heavy).

Your body gives you messages continuously. It's up to you to learn how to receive and acknowledge them. The body speaks to you through flutters and whimpers. It's as uncomplicated as feeling good or not feeling good. Knowing how your body spoke to you when you asked and heard yourself say "I'm single" is extremely powerful. From this insight, you can learn how to decode the message it has given you.

Let me explain more about how this all works. Emotions are extraordinarily complex, and they have mental and physical components. Your body responds to the way you feel, how you act, and what you think. This is often referred to as the mind-body connection. You've all experienced it. When you are happy, you breathe in long deep breaths, your shoulders are relaxed, and you generally don't feel pain in your body. But if we tip to the other end of the scale, where you are feeling constant stress, how does your body respond? Your breathing becomes shallow, your muscles tense, and your shoulders lift up closer to your ears.

How do you think this affects your body over time? Nervous stomach, headaches, and grinding your teeth are all stress-related symptoms. Isn't it flabbergasting that we choose to continue to ignore them, popping pretty little pills and wishing them away? You instinctively relate past experiences with a specific emotion, and they all find a way to express themselves in your body. All you need to do is learn how to pay attention.

I'm not a therapist and will never claim to be one, but I will share my findings as an avid people watcher and life coach. I have found the way to set yourself free from the nasty stuff is to know how you feel at all times—and by being aware of what is going on emotionally within you. If you continue to choose to ignore your feelings, they will find new ways to come back and poke you in order to get your attention later.

So where did you feel it? Did you feel a tightening in your chest, a sinking feeling in your stomach, or perhaps a lump in your throat?

A Feeling in Your Chest

Do you accept yourself for who you are or do you lack self-love? Maybe you are feeling particularly unloved, rejected, or abandoned? This was exactly how I felt when I first ended my marriage. Do you feel a lack of freedom in your life? Perhaps you have an unusually heavy heart at the moment and are having a hard time adapting? Does this sound correct?

A Lump or Dryness in Your Throat

Do you feel as though you did not adequately represent yourself in the breakup with your ex? Was there something you would like to have said or still feel the need to say? Is financial security and having nice possessions a concern? How about trust? Is there someone in your life you can trust without a doubt? Do you hold back tears and swallow your pain? Sound familiar?

A Fluttering In Your Solar Plexus (The Pit of Your Stomach)

When you said, "I'm single," did it feel as though something dropped into your stomach. Since you've been on your own, do you feel unworthy and a lot less confident? Are you questioning how you will get by on your own? Do you find you are unable to focus and concentrate and have a difficult time making decisions? Is your biggest fear being alone?

These questions may seem rather odd to ask yourself; however, it's essential that you identify where you are holding pain and suffering in your body. Knowing this will support you in moving forward. Having an awareness of where thoughts and feelings manifest in your body is essential to your overall health. For example, if you are holding your pain in your solar plexus, this could cause an ulcer, a nervous stomach, or even anxiety.

It's sad that we have not been taught to connect in this way with our bodies. Remember when I said that deep breathing dissipates tension? Well, it's the perfect remedy. Relaxation and tension cannot coexist in your body at the same time. Shallow breathing means you are tense; take three deep breaths in and change the patterns in your body.

Here are some breathing exercises to do depending on where you felt something in your body.

If you felt something in your chest, take a deep breath in and focus on your lungs. Count to three, open your mouth, and release your breath quickly. Repeat this exercise three times, or for as many times as you like, to break up tension in your chest. How does your body feel differently? Make notes in your journal.

If you felt something in your throat, open your mouth wide, take a deep breath in while focusing on your throat, hold it for a count of three, and let it out, making an "ah" sound. Acknowledge your throat where you are storing anger, sadness, or grief, and give it lots of air. Deep breathing provides a release in your throat.

If you have been keeping your words to yourself lately, you have not had the opportunity to speak your truth. You may feel the need to cry. Simply let your tears flow. Crying is a natural function that helps the body relieve stress, but many of us are often discouraged from doing so. In the same way that perspiring is the body's natural function to keep from overheating, the natural way to relieve anxiety and stress is to cry.

If you felt something in your solar plexus or the pit of your stomach, stand and put your hands on your stomach. Take three deep breaths in, all the way down into your solar plexus, expanding it fully while focusing your attention on filling up your belly. Then release your breath as slowly as possible. Take your time. Do you feel the difference in your body? Some of you may even find this release causes you to cry. This is perfectly okay. Go ahead and give your body the release it requires.

One last time, say out loud, "I'm single." Can you feel where it sits in your body now? If not, keep saying this out loud until you do—and refer to the corresponding breathing exercise above. Once you are aware of where the heaviness is in your body, take a few minutes to jot down any feelings, emotions, thoughts, or visions that come to you. Do you feel empty, deflated, overwhelmed, scared, unsure, or anxious? I felt an overwhelming sense of abandonment spreading itself like thick lard in my solar plexus area. It felt heavy, as though it would take a herculean effort to get rid of.

Over the years, I played my share of silly games with my ex. I made him promise to never leave me and tell me that we would grow old together. I never truly believed this mouthful of security was possible. For many years, I worried about being abandoned and never felt as though anyone honestly had my back. And now, that is exactly what I have created in my life. I had bought into the idea that I wasn't worthy of having anyone who genuinely loved me. I take total responsibility for my part in the destruction of our relationship, but I still can't help feeling abandoned. When I don't listen to my body's messages, these feelings often manifest in my dreams. In my dream world, I am often caged and cannot escape, about to be captured, or running away from something. Do you find your dreams are also plagued by your anxieties?

I have come to understand that the secret to everything of any importance in my life comes down to how I feel at any given moment. Acknowledging those feelings is particularly important. Give them attention—and consciously choose to let them go. Shifting into better feelings is the key to my well-being and can be yours as well.

I was not shy about asking myself how I felt as I gazed up at my bedroom ceiling each night, and in fact I still do to this day. Did the thought running through my head feel heavy or light? I knew I had the answers to all of my questions. After all, who knew me better than I did? My girlfriends could only offer advice from their own points of view—not from mine. I simply had to learn to trust in myself and relax in order to receive the guidance I was seeking. Take a walk and get out of your head, and suddenly other possibilities will reveal themselves. It's that distraction thing again.

One of the first steps to embracing being single again, after all that you have been through with the separation, is to begin from right where you are. You have been through a lot, and it doesn't seem to make much sense or feel fair, but you've lived through it. If you are reading this book, perhaps you have become inspired to remember who you truly are. You simply wouldn't have led yourself to me if you weren't.

Let's start again. Take a long deep breath in and say, "I'm single." Feel where those words trigger a fluttering, a sinking feeling, a tightness, or emptiness in your body. Play with your ability to recognize how you feel and where it manifests in your body. Do not beat yourself up for feeling this way.

What did you feel? What words came to mind? What did you feel in your belly? Was it anger? Perfect. Anger is where you start from then. Was it loneliness? Perfect. Then feeling lonely is where you start from. Were you depressed? Perfect. Acknowledge this feeling and create from there. Are you catching on yet?

Thank your body for the message it is sharing with you. It's extremely easy, but you like to complicate it. Don't. Merely get in touch with, and accept, how you feel at this moment. Don't hold on to it; simply give it a moment of your undivided attention. If a feeling is bubbling up inside of you, it's worth paying attention to.

Say, "Yes! I do feel I've been dumped! I do feel I've been taken advantage of! I do feel unloved right now! I am upset with how this turned out and don't feel I deserve what happened to me!"

Call it what it is! You deserve to give this to yourself; do not deny how you feel because you believe you are supposed to feel some other way. Let go of everyone else's expectations of you. You are not here to live up to anyone's expectations except your own. You are an incredible woman who has ideas, inspiration, sex appeal, and moxie!

One-Week Emotional Body Connection Exercise

Here's a fun exercise for you. For one week—seven full days— practice these five steps at the beginning and end of your day.

1) As soon as you wake up, while still in bed, ask yourself how you feel. Open your journal and immediately write down your findings. This is about getting in touch with your emotions. Before you get out of bed, put your hands over your heart and ask, "How do I feel right now?"

   Are you feeling lost? Could it be that you are overwhelmed with so much unknown out in front of you? Relax, feel it, and open your heart to owning this feeling.

   Once you have a good idea of how you are feeling, sit quietly for three minutes and simply allow yourself to feel this way. Give any thoughts and emotions that bubble up your full attention. Following this, write any emotions, gut feelings, words, thoughts, or visions that came to you in a journal, including the date and time.

2) Rate how you feel between one and ten.
      1 = cynical and negative
      2= overwhelmed and irritated
      3= disappointed and frustrated
      4= doubtful and worried

5= discouraged and hopeless
6= angry and vengeful
7= jealous
8= insecure and unworthy
9= fearful and powerless
10= call someone for help

If you do this exercise for a few days and keep scoring a ten, I suggest you seek professional help. Visit your doctor and ask to be referred to someone who can help you move forward. You can also seek out a spiritual coach or a life coach.

Record this number in your journal along with the emotions attached to the number listed above. Each number, moving up the list from ten to one, feels lighter than the last. Feeling powerless is much heavier than feeling negative and cynical. If you find the emotions you are recording are not on the list—like optimistic, empowered, happy, relaxed, bored, or content—you have indeed begun to let go of a good portion of the heaviness, and you should be feeling much freer.

3) At this point, put your hands over your heart, inhale deeply, and hold it for a count of three. Let it out through your mouth, releasing a hefty sigh of relief, and say, "Ah!" Repeat this exercise twice.

4) Once you've cycled through the first three steps three times, say "Thank you" and "I love you" out loud and smile. Even if you have to force a smile onto your face, plaster it on. You have no idea what a smile does to the endorphins in your body—smile no matter how fake it feels.

5) When you have your hands over your heart, are feeling what you are feeling, and have a large grin on your face, shift your

thoughts to something joyful. It could be the taste of your favorite cookie, a good laugh you recently experienced, or a wonderful past memory (that does not include your ex!). It doesn't matter what thought you conjure up—as long as it feels good. Stay in that space for as long as you can. Feel your body shift into joy.

Each day, find more thoughts to make you smile. On day one, find one thought to smile about. On day two, find two. On day three, find three ... and so on. If it is undoubtedly your desire to have more joy in your life, your job is to create it.

This exercise, done regularly, will assist you in acknowledging your emotional body. Being single means being with you most of the time. For example, for the past two days, I have been on my own. My son was out with his father, and my friends were all doing their own thing. It was just Chester Pug and me.

When you're by yourself, after being with someone for years, even if they weren't always in your personal space, you were never really alone. It can be difficult being on your own with no one around. Many of you may have never experienced being with yourself for any long period of time. Perhaps you lived with your parents, then maybe with a roommate, or went to school where you were surrounded by people. When have you ever been on your own? So you have to get acquainted with you again. It's critical now, I assure you. If you don't, you are going to continue to barf all over everyone.

It's difficult to move beyond nasty feelings if you keep reinventing new ones.

The way to step past nasty feelings is to acknowledge them, admit how you feel, give these feelings the attention they deserve, and let them go. I know, I know ... the "let them go" part is where we struggle most. However, how is it possible for new experiences to flow into your life if you are holding on to past memories that don't make you happy? So plaster a smile on your face and give more and more of your energy and attention to thoughts that make you feel good. I'm not saying you will unexpectedly find yourself grinning from ear to ear, feeling all joyful and happy. Going from anger or depression to joy is a significant jump. Humans function better when we take smaller steps. But you can move from anger into discouragement once you give it some attention—and then from discouragement to blame. Although these still feel like nasty emotions, each is a step toward joy. When you deny your feelings, you stay right where you are.

The secret is to recognize what negative emotions are popping up and destroy your attachment to them. Can you recall a time when you were upset and ignored it, only later to have it chew its way back into your thoughts when another circumstance triggered the memory? It's your body's natural way of talking to you. If you choose to keep ignoring these emotions, they will keep popping up—often when you don't want them to. Continuing to push your feelings aside will cause your body to resort to *pain* in order to get your attention.

You need to get connected ... with you.

You've spent your life disconnecting from everything you are passionate about. You have allowed others to make important decisions and choices for you (which is also a choice). You have done what's best for everyone else, thinking this is the only option or the only way your life can be. You've got to stop now! This is your life—not anyone else's. If you have children with you, what example are you setting for them by barfing all over everyone you talk to and being angry, dysfunctional or unmotivated? How is not paying attention to the way you feel going make you feel better? Sooner or later, your emotions will erupt. I promise you. They may erupt in a breakdown—or you could become extremely sick. Do you see how silly it is to deny looking after yourself first?

You are #1 in your life.
Everything is about you first.

You really have to embrace what it feels like to be a bit selfish. Being selfish does not mean being rude to others or altogether ignoring people's interests, opinions, and needs. My definition of being selfish is doing my best to relate to the needs and wishes of friends and family members while knowing where to draw the line when it infringes upon my own best interests.

Being there for someone does not include feeling their pain, but that appears to be what is expected. Many cannot comprehend how someone can understand their pain without actually feeling it. By asking this of you, they most likely have no desire to move forward into new possibilities. They aren't open to the idea that anything sensational could be possible. Loving them, listening to them, encouraging them, or distracting them are all better ways to help them shift from depression to joy. Wouldn't you agree? Pity parties are of no good to anyone.

A dear friend came to me regularly for guidance and love—and to barf. She was entangled in an intensely frustrating relationship and was sharing the upsetting experience of a recent trip with her boyfriend. I did my best to help her acknowledge and release the blame she was torturing herself with. Unfortunately, she was far too upset by what had happened and couldn't hear anything I was saying. She was determined to make me understand that what her boyfriend had done was unacceptable, disrespectful, and dangerous. As I listened, she repeatedly poured out her pain, disgust, and fear to me, always insisting that I did not understand how afraid she was for her life!

Suddenly I knew why she repeatedly shared her discomfort—she wanted me to feel her pain. From her perspective, I only appeared to be listening to her story. She desired a sympathetic reaction that proved I related to her pain. Little did she know that I am quite skilled in the art of detachment. My brain was churning away, analyzing her pure vibe, reading her body language, listening to every word she chose to express her frustrations, feeling her emotionally, and reading everything between the lines. I was doing what I do—reading her energy to help her discover old patterns and beliefs that were holding her in this painful experience—so I could later lead her toward better feelings. While she wanted to relive her experience and share the horrific events with a friend, in order for us to bond in some way, I was looking for new possibilities. I was moving forward, and she was stuck in her painful story.

Finally, I stopped her and said, "I know exactly how you feel. You are pissed off at what he did, and you were terrified and humiliated. What you want me to do is agree that what he did was unacceptable. You want me to justify the way you are feeling by agreeing with you so you can feel better."

"Yes, yes!" she replied, finally relieved that I understood.

This is how we are conditioned to relate to each other—and why we repeat our sad stories to everyone who will listen. We tell our stories again and again as a way to lash out because it is a method of vengeance. We position ourselves as righteous victims to reveal the other people as the aggressors.

Can you see now how being there for someone does not mean feeling their pain? Who cares how the dictionary defines the word *selfish*. I say ... redefine it and make it work for you. What else is possible for this word? How much more can it be if we allow it? Get *self-ish* (expose all of who you really are), and you will discover you have so much more to give to your children, your friends, your family, and the world. Life is all about relationships, and you can't build strong, healthy relationships if you do not have a good relationship with you first.

Now is you time. Do the One-Week Emotional Body Connection Exercise and see what changes occur within you. All choices ahead of you are yours to make, enjoy, and receive. You don't have to check in with anyone—unless you're thinking of moving to another city with your kids. Then I suggest you pick up the phone and talk to your ex. I'm talking about the simple daily decisions. You are not required to check in with your spouse or get his approval any longer. You don't have to discuss the meals for the week. There are no worries around upsetting anyone's schedule; if you want to sign up for a new class, go for it. This is your life now, and you get to run the show. Can you imagine what else could be possible? Now—more than ever—it's important to pay attention to how you feel.

Becoming a married woman happened overnight. After your wedding, do you remember how you had to keep telling yourself you were no longer single? Do you recall repeating your new name and feeling proud? When hugging your new hubby, did you say, "I'm

Mrs. X!" and feel like a new woman? After the party was over, life began to feel sort of routine again. Becoming a married woman was a big transition—and so is the transition into singledom.

Embracing being single means you are adapting to a new way of living, including new routines and possibilities. This isn't anything you haven't done before. Smile a little more often, step into more of your own amazingness, and cut those butt-cords that are connecting you to all the thoughts holding you in fear and disempowerment. Open your eyes to now—going forward as a Single Goddess.

Chapter Five
BEGIN BY REINVENTING YOURSELF

Transitioning from being married to single can be compared to turning a huge ship around in water. It can take a while to get moving in a new direction. Through the process of turning this ship around, you may have resisted, fought, and made waves. I used to think of myself as the ship fighting against the water as I did my best to turn my life in a new direction.

One day a brilliant girlfriend of mine said, "Catherine, don't be the ship. Be the water."

Suddenly it all made sense. A lot of changes were occurring in my work environment. The turmoil I was experiencing there was like a tidal wave rolling out across all the other parts of my life. Sound familiar? I was so unhappy that most of my days ended in tears. I continually begged my ex for permission to quit my job. I simply needed to know I had his support. I desperately wanted to be saved from that toxic environment.

When I was able to step back and see the bigger picture unfolding, I could see my work environment was a playground I was learning from. But when immersed in it, I did not like the person I transformed into. In addition, my ex and I had fallen out of love, and I was ashamed to admit failing at my marriage. Although I had known in my heart for years that he no longer loved me, a piece of me was too proud to admit I was about to be abandoned again. We both knew our relationship was finished. I hated that I was about to declare that my husband and I would not grow old together as we had planned.

Once the decision to separate was made, things happened quickly. Stop all engines and coast to a halt. Within two weeks, I found and rented an apartment for my son and me, and the packing began. Turn the rudders in a new direction. My ex and I quickly—and without any fighting—decided who would get what. We divided our belongings as I packed. Restart engines. I simply wanted to get out fast, and find my way through this to whatever was ahead. Begin the transition to a new direction.

This clunky process of stopping and starting is so much easier from the perspective of being water. Water flows. Water bends. Water caresses the objects moving through it, making room for them. This was what my friend meant when she said I was the water and not the ship. When that huge, massive ship came to a halt, the water around it simply adjusted and waited patiently. When the ship began to move and push its way in a new direction, water flowed effortlessly with its movements.

Most times, I believe I did think, feel, and act like water. Before I knew it, my son and I were unpacked and living in our new home. I did not want to hurt my ex. I still respect him and always will. Love him? No. Respect him? Yes. He is a wonderful man, and I will always wish the best for him and hope he continues to be my friend. I did not want to be the ship, pushing through the water, breaking the waves, and fighting the current. That was what I had been doing for ten years. From that point forward, it was time to be water—flowing, flexible, gentle, and free.

At one time, returning to singledom was a thought, an option that crossed your mind. You had hoped it would never come to fruition. But it did. Your life may have been drastically altered, but you begin the journey of reinventing it, stepping into bigger possibilities of who you are. Say, "I wonder what amazing adventures await me?" Open your heart to receive all that comes your way. When most of us ask ourselves such an open-ended question, we start conjuring conclusions. What if there were no conclusions? What if you didn't have to come up with a list of possible outcomes?

Before you can create or reinvent anything new in your life, there is a need to become aware of and strip away some of the conclusions you have bought into. You're like a little pressure cooker of thoughts, beliefs, emotions, and stories that constantly spin you in different directions. All those details cloud your truth and your real knowing.

Here are a few questions to ask yourself:

- If I was not afraid of any specific outcome, what is one thing I would do right now that would empower me?
- What have-to thoughts am I holding on to that are actually keeping me stuck? (I have to do _____. I have to make sure this gets done first).
- What am I afraid to do because I worry others will judge me?

You are holding on to a lot of limiting beliefs and definitions about life in general. Your true desire is to move forward, but conclusions, have-to thoughts, and judgments hold you stuck.

Reinventing yourself is not about tearing down walls as if you are a madwoman on a mission.

I've seen the reinventing process attempted in this mad teardown manner—only to watch it cause more harm. You have probably done enough tearing apart during this process to last a lifetime. Deconstructing is probably a better word to describe what you need to do. Take one brick down every day and replace it with one that makes you feel better.

Tearing Down the Wall of Shame

Here is an exercise for you to play with to help you let go of some of these restrictions. While taking your shower tomorrow, imagine the shower stall as a brick wall you have constructed around yourself. Envision that the bricks in this wall include every negative feeling and emotion you're experiencing right now. Close your eyes and envision reaching out and removing one of the bricks. Holding it in your hands, notice the word *lack* stamped on each of its six sides. Imagine how pleasant and light it would feel to remove this heavy brick of lack from your life completely. Take a moment and consider why you might have chosen to surround yourself with lack. Ask how lack has served you. What does living from lack provide? What do you love about lack?

For example, I choose to surround myself with lack and love it because:

- It makes me feel better when I blame my ex for taking possessions I felt were not his.

- It gives me a reason to feel robbed of a future.
- It allows me to appear to be the good guy in our break-up when I explain to people why I didn't take the _____ and let him have it.

Don't spend a huge amount of time conjuring an excess of negative thoughts to support lack. Three points are enough. You've already supported these negative thoughts long enough and given those nasty buggers a lot of attention. In fact, as you are thinking these negative thoughts, you may notice your breathing becoming more rapid, your lips pursing, and your body tensing. We don't want this reaction, especially when you are enjoying a nice relaxing shower to begin your day. Your objective is to remove one nasty brick from your wall of shame—and replace it with one that serves you now.

What should you replace this lack brick with? Abundance, of course! Imagine a new brick that is made completely of air. Air is flexible, flowing, and transparent—and it accepts change. On each side of this light, airy brick, imagine writing the word abundance while making a statement out loud (yes, as you are showering) that supports abundance in your life. This will total six abundance statements, ladies. We came up with three nasties to support lack, but now you are going to counteract them with six goodies! Here are a couple, but I'm not going to take all the fun away from you:

- I have the most amazing friends—and even more time to spend with them!
- I have the whole bed to myself. I can hog all the sheets and all the pillows and make it look any way I want!

It doesn't matter how silly your ideas of abundance sound. This is about awakening a new perspective within you.

I chose to have you do this exercise during your morning shower because of the nature of thoughts typically dancing around in your head at this time. If you were to pay attention to the thoughts swirling around during this time, you would hear a lot of yesterday's news. They consist of facts, circumstances, situations, events, and incidents that occurred yesterday—in your past. If yesterday's news is not on your mind, I'll bet you are worrying about something you have to do in the near future. Both come from the lack of something. Your thoughts are generated by the lack of what didn't happen yesterday, or they are focused on something that has not yet happened in your future. Each binds you to lack.

Start playing this new game in the shower every morning. You can choose to work on one brick a week if you wish, or one a day. Here are some other bricks to remove, relabel, and support:

- threats
- guilt
- unworthiness
- inadequacy
- betrayal
- fear
- shame
- anger

It won't take you long to flip this wall of shame into one you will be happy to claim!

Are the exercises I'm providing throughout this book corny and silly? Yes, some of them are! Girl, you need to get corny and silly and engage in some kooky exercises. You are on a quest to lighten up! Life is not supposed to be a struggle. Life is not about working hard and beating yourself down to a place of pain and suffering in order to gain entry through pearly gates upon your exit. Exiting is not the focus here. You came here to live! It's that simple. I'm sure you've got those butt cheeks of yours clenched tight and your shoulders pushed up so high they are trying to connect themselves to your earlobes from the stress you have been feeding your body. Stop it! Play along with my silly games and wake up to your amazing electric potential. Your electricity (or your passion) is not driven from lack or pain and suffering. Your electricity resides in a joyful, loving place within you, but you have forgotten it is even there. Stop fooling yourself and try to have some fun with this transition.

As I moved into this single, forty-plus territory, I made it a mission to pay attention to my emotions. I checked in with myself regularly to ensure that I was always aware of how I was feeling. I still practice this process because it fuels my passions. I cannot impress upon you enough how important it is to know how you feel at all times. It's critical to be aware of which emotions are driving your thoughts and contributing to your decisions. Going with the flow does not mean being a pushover. Putting the blame on others and saying they are taking advantage of you is not a good reaction either.

For some reason, we as a culture have adopted blame as a method we use to feel better about the choices we make, rather than taking responsibility for them.

I understand why people use blame. It's a learned skill passed down from previous generations that requires very little skill to learn to employ. I'll also bet there is a lot of blame associated with your breakup.

In my own personal example, I knew I had changed my point of view and opinions about what I desired in life. The new ideas and concepts I shared with my ex only bored and confused him. Thank goodness I had discovered the benefits of paying attention to my emotions. I was able to identify how I was feeling throughout this process, using the techniques shared in this book, and they stopped me from waving the finger of blame at my ex.

It's important get in touch with your emotions. Why would such things be a part of who you are if they were not meant to provide you some sort of assistance? We don't ignore the messages provided to us by sight, sound, taste, or touch. It doesn't make sense to ignore your feelings. I remember crying at night in my new apartment, thinking that I might live out the rest of my life without a man loving me. I felt so alone at times, but I gave my feelings my undivided attention and reached for better ones. This was how I pulled myself through this experience, and this is what I hope I am encouraging you to do.

This practice was like a lifeline I held on to while I was down in that hole of desperation and grief. My coworkers and friends would tell you a different story of how I left my ex in record time and started my new life. This of course, was exactly what I wanted the outside world to see. My wall of shame was built well, and I even fooled myself into believing it was protection instead of something I was hiding behind.

My quest in any problem I encounter is to get in touch with how it is making me feel before I reach out to others for answers. One trick I use when I find myself pointing a nasty finger of blame is to turn that finger around and point it back at myself. Everywhere I am blaming outside sources for my misfortune is turned back on myself. This isn't about placing blame on myself; in fact it is about taking control and responsibility for how I perceive what I am experiencing.

Working internally can be more empowering than asking others for advice. Don't get me wrong. It is important to engage in conversation outside of yourself about what bothers you. It's part of being human. We all have a need to use our voices in order to connect with our emotions. In fact, our voices are vibrations of who we are. Hearing our thoughts and feelings verbally helps us digest, acknowledge, and accept what we are experiencing. Instead of simply barfing all over everyone or begging for answers, turn these conversations inward to better understand your feelings. This way, when you do reach out for assistance, you will be ready to receive other possibilities. Keep the barfing to yourself as best you can— until you are actually ready to receive support and guidance.

When you are barfing, you are not looking for a solution. You are simply reacting. That little monster of an ego is hurt and wants attention. It likes to hear your sad story over and over and over again, and it urges you to share it with as many people as possible. So feed it. Sit down alone and tell it the story of how you are feeling, thank it for listening, and then send it on its way. Take a deep breath in and shift out of that negative story. You will be in a more empowering place and able to talk to your friends—or seek help from a professional— but talk while progressively moving in a forward direction.

It's Time to Get Excited

What is there to get excited about? Just about everything!

- You have the rest of your life in front of you. Oh yeah—that's good! I know you can't see this from where you are right now, but you will when you are ready to choose to.

- You are open to becoming more aware of your feelings and moving toward better ones. If you aren't, you would have thrown this book down long ago. Stop fighting it.
- You get to rediscover yourself. Most married women never fully get this opportunity. They may have a partner who objects to the idea of them expanding their ways of thinking. They often don't explore themselves as much as they would if they had no one to report to. We change as we grow (notice I didn't say age). If you have the same exact beliefs and values now as when you were twenty, you would do yourself a huge favor by reviewing them. It's amazing what you uncover when you dig into your core beliefs and ask yourself if they are serving you in a positive way. We often discover that core beliefs are having the opposite effect on us; they are stopping us from doing what we would enjoy.
- You get to joyfully remember who you are. This is the best gift of all.
- You get to decide what makes you feel good—and do it.

This is exciting stuff, ladies. Remembering and reinventing yourself means you get to recall everything you are passionate about—and make those passions your new focus. Imagine rediscovering what lights a fire in your belly and doing it just for the fun of it.

There are so many outstanding qualities about you that you have forgotten exist and allowed to slip away. You've buried them because you thought you had to act a specific way to impress other people. You created a persona for that. At work, you act appropriately, which actually means you follow someone else's rules. You created a persona for that. How about your family members? How do you act around them? This is a sticky one for me. I love my family, but when my brother and mother are involved, things usually go awry. I'm never truly sure what happens, but it always ends on a bad note with me feeling like an idiot for having spoken out or acted like a fool. I have embarrassed myself in the past on way too many occasions. Depending on the dynamics of your family environment, you have created a persona for that. How about your friends? How do you act around them? What personas have you created to be with each of them?

Who are you? How would you know with all of these different personas acting in your place? They are like guards you have created to protect you. Unfortunately, they are actually keeping you hidden—even from yourself.

It's just you now; the greatest gift you can give yourself is to become more acquainted with you. The secret to reinventing yourself is not to change everything about you in one fell swoop but to rediscover pieces of you a little bit at a time. Have fun slowly exchanging those bricks for positive, loving ones.

What about you never changes? What physically has been the same for the past five years? How have you been the same emotionally for the past five years? Which relationships are draining you? You could begin by simply getting a new haircut or reading a book that is normally out of character for you. Start looking around, ladies. You are not alone.

At this moment, I am typing on my computer on the patio of a coffee shop. Two ladies at the table beside me are single. One appears to be over sixty, and the other is most likely my age. Single women over forty are everywhere. Right here on this patio, there are five people—and three of us are single women over forty!

Last night I was walking Chester Pug and met up with another single woman in my complex. Because she too was walking her dog, we immediately connected. She shared how grateful she was to have her little furry friend living with her now that she is on own. I was walking my dog with a total stranger who lives in the same complex and has a remarkably similar life. She shared her story of recently being divorced, how she was coping with being on her own again, and how different single life was for her.

Look around. You are far from being alone or the first person who has ever experienced separation or divorce. My gorgeous friend, you can be one of the few who embrace this new beginning—and fall in love with yourself again. It all depends on your perspective.

Chapter Six
IS IT REAL? CAN I TOUCH IT?

Let's talk about this whole reality thing. The word *thing* is perhaps a better description of the word reality.

Thing: An entity, idea, or a quality perceived, known, or thought to have its own existence.

Reality, on the other hand, is defined as *a quality or state of being; actual or true*. I want to know who decides what is actual or true— and what isn't. I believe that how much influence this word has is highly overrated. This one word alone has enough power to hold people in a state of complete disempowerment.

I find words very interesting. Over time, they sometimes adopt new flavors. In the same way new slang words incessantly infiltrate the

English language, we also manipulate other words, giving them hidden agendas. Don't you love how we do this?

How you define your reality is actually quite complex and unique. Using your senses, you evaluate something new and then call upon your past experiences and beliefs to create a definition. For every sight, sound, taste, feeling, and experience, we conjure our own realities from our individual definitions. How can there be such a thing as one reality?

Interestingly, we also willingly, and without question, adopt how someone else defines their truth or reality as our own. We toss the word *reality* around like a dagger, and we throw it at anyone we decide is messing up the agreed upon order of things.

If someone tells me to wake up and face reality, are they being kind and helping to point me in the direction of empowerment? Or is it their intention to shake my sensibility back to the familiar pattern of what is considered normal? This word-dagger is a manipulation tool used to put people back on course with what society has been taught is acceptable. They actually want to say, "Catherine, stop living in a dream world—and get back to work like the rest of us!"

It's remarkable what comes to mind when most of us think of the phrase "facing reality." I envision a limited environment where I have no control. Facing reality feels like someone saying, "This is the way it is—and I can't do anything about it." What images and thoughts come to mind for you?

We all came here to experience life and grow as individuals. If everything we saw was set in stone, nothing would ever change. There would be no visionaries or entrepreneurs. We know humans have changed drastically since our ancestors first stood upright. Their reality was completely different from how many perceive reality today. This means reality is not constant; it is always changing. For some reason though, we go along with the idea that this as the way it is. It's quite confusing for me! Do you feel confused?

Times Change

Today while standing in line for my morning latte, I overheard two mothers discussing cell phones.

One of the women said, "I think kids grow up too fast these days. What happened to the time when kids played outside, climbed trees, and used their imaginations? Why does a nine-year-old need a cell phone?"

I completely understood her point of view. Kids today are almost born with technology in their hands. They are punching away on a keyboard and using a mouse by the time they are five—sometimes even earlier. Not so long ago, the vast majority didn't even have a computer, let alone a cell phone.

This conversation was the perfect example of how times change. I poked my nose into their conversation (one of my favorite things to do) and said, "I bet every generation has said that about the next. Wouldn't you agree?" Both women agreed.

What does this have to do with reality? Things change. Nothing stays the same for very long. This includes what is transpiring in your life. Each new generation has a different set of ideas about what is cool, hip, trendy, or acceptable. The fact that my generation played outside, climbed trees, and played hopscotch doesn't mean that how this generation spends their free time is wrong.

Children today are living completely different lives than children from my generation, and I can guarantee my mother's generation was vastly different than the reality of my youth. No generation ever fully understands the motivations of the next. For some reason, how we used to do things always seems to be the best way, doesn't it? What a wonderful world it would be if everyone did what I thought was right. Life would be so much easier, don't you agree? I'm sure if it makes me happy, everyone else will be happy too. Are you with me? Does this work for you? No, probably not.

When I ask women who are newly separated to share their definition of reality, the response is often not positive. When you get separated or divorced, the reality is:

- you're all alone
- you have no one to help you
- you have to take care of your children all by yourself
- you have to pay all the bills, which is a struggle for a single woman
- you can't get sick because there is no one to take care of you
- you've ruined your children's lives and have scarred them forever
- you're a failure because your marriage ended

If this is the reality of a newly single, forty-plus, separated woman, it's a wonder we can even get dressed in the morning! Where is the fun in living this reality? How can we make those statements knowing they are not 100 percent true? Why are some people so determined to live this reality if it's so darn crappy?

Have you ever noticed those who say "Reality is" repeatedly in conversations are generally not happy people? The next time you hear someone using this term, pay attention. It's an incredibly misused term. Many will use this limiting term when they actually want to say, "In the past, this is how it happened. I have proof to show you the way it is. What I have experienced to be truth is that life is always crappy. Put away your rose-colored glasses." Others want to say, "You're wrong." Do you know what I mean?

It's quite difficult as an individual to move forward into a fresh new positive environment if we are stuck in a reality where we believe we have no control.

People with this belief usually focus on past negative experiences. Some would even call this living from the ego. Perhaps they have no idea how to observe the world through rose-colored glasses. In fact, I bet they have no desire to. They aren't visionaries, although many own businesses, which amazes me. They prefer to base their choices on statistics and what they know. Out of habit, they plug into their egos and recall past events, using them as the facts to prove their current realities.

I understand why businesses use facts and figures to make future projections. After all, it's what their investors expect of them. In a person's everyday life though, this way of thinking doesn't allow for any creative thought. Even in the business world, it only allows the projection of a percentage increase. It's quite difficult, as an individual, to move forward into a fresh, new, positive environment if we are stuck in a reality where we believe we have no control.

By now, some of you are joyfully shaking your fingers at me and wishing you could tell me all about your reality. If you have bought into a static reality, and want to stay there, all the power to you. However, I am curious to know why you would choose to defend something that does not promote joy in your life.

Saying, "Reality is ..." is a complete showstopper. These two words alone can stop all creative thinking in its tracks.

"This is the way it is and there is nothing I can do about it." Saying that—or believing that—makes it tremendously difficult to attempt any kind of creative thinking. In this moment, this is the way it appears to be; in the next moment, it will be something completely different and unique.

For quite some time, I have enjoyed the process of changing what I used to think was my static reality and the ways in which I limited myself. I've become aware of how easy it is to allow negative mind chatter to consume us. Our thoughts have amazing power. Have you ever tried to not think a thought? It's pretty hard, isn't it? Try not to think about a book. What just popped into your thoughts?

The ego likes to conjure up past examples and experiences to show us how we've already experienced something—and to help us decide how to proceed in any new situation. That negative mind chatter is your ego.

After separating from my ex, the first man I had a significant relationship with viewed the world with what I would consider a limiting point of view. In the beginning of our relationship, he presented himself as being extremely open-minded, but it didn't take me long to figure out where he placed limitations on himself—and on other people. Germs and sickness were the first red flags I received that we were going to be out of sync with each other.

One afternoon while Christmas shopping, we stepped onto an escalator. I grabbed the handrail to steady myself. It's a pretty common thing to do. I was in my own little world of Christmas shopping bliss when a thunderous voice behind me demanded that I remove my hand from the rail.

"Catherine, do you have any idea how many people have spread their germs onto that! Don't you know how dirty it is?" He quickly and forcefully freed my hand from the disgustingly dirty rail.

Ego Mind Chatter: "Don't you remember your mother telling you that where you find large numbers of people, you find a host of germs?"

He also shared his limited reality way of thinking while I was heating a cup of tea in the microwave. The microwave was stationed at the same level as my head. I put in my cup of tea, punched in the numbers, and watched as it spun to toasty hotness. This was not acceptable behavior! Standing about three feet behind me, he lunged and grabbed me, pulling me out of harm's way!

I was quite startled and looked to him for an explanation, which I quickly received.

"Don't you know the brain damage those things can cause? Do you want a brain tumor? Don't ever put your head close to microwaves! I don't ever want to lose you!"

I was at a loss for words. When I asked why this flipped him out so much, it was apparent he thought his actions were protecting me from danger. This was his way of showing love. I knew the relationship was not going in a joyful direction.

Ego Mind Chatter: "Remember when you read that article about what microwave exposure can do to people?"

This was just the tip of the iceberg. He also said, "In reality, the successes of my children are a direct reflection of me. They must make choices I feel are good ones in order for me to feel good about what people think of me."

Ego Mind Chatter: "We don't like to be judged."

"In reality, we have to do things we don't like in order to live a good life."

Ego Mind Chatter: "Hard work is always rewarded."

I definitely don't want to play in his definition of reality. Most people have certain chores they don't really enjoy. For example, I prefer to vacuum the house, I and hate doing laundry. If we could see that doing those chores made us feel good later, perhaps we wouldn't dislike them so much. They would feel like natural occurrences, and we wouldn't charge doing them with so much negative energy. Individual perspective creates how we feel about our current reality. What is your definition of a good life?

The relationship was an amazing experience with many hidden gems. When I reflect on the choices, actions, and decisions I made, one of the wonderful gems showed me I can never stop being who I am in order to fit into someone else's life and reality. Does this mean I will never engage in another male-female relationship? No.

Unfortunately though, fitting ourselves into other people's lives is very common.

I have discovered I will not silence my feelings because they are not what someone else chooses. This includes all relationships. The right man will be attracted to me. Although this man and I had much in common in regard to the types of foods we ate, the climates we enjoyed, and the stores we enjoyed shopping in—all of which gave us an initial impression that we had much in common—we were worlds apart. I fell in love with him very quickly because of these similarities, but I soon began spending more time fighting to change reality than I was embracing it and going with the flow.

Is it possible for you to wrap your head around the idea that everything is temporary? What if everything you are living and experiencing right now, which seems so real and limiting, could change in the blink of an eye?

Your ego wants you to think otherwise. That silly mind chatter is always working to lead you back to familiar patterns, telling you how crappy your life is right now. Ego only knows what it sees and has experienced. It also believes other people's experiences are the way it is and assumes they are your truth. This primitive part of you is helpful when used properly to make decisions. Ego pays attention to everyone else's business instead of your own. It loves worry, rejection, and familiar patterns.

Letting go of these limiting patterns will benefit you as you reinvent yourself. Life is always changing. Believe your life can be joyful and full of love—and look for fresh new experiences to prove that every day. You are the constant creator of your reality.

You don't need to learn how to speed up what you are creating in order to get to what you think is the end result. Instead, pay attention to how much each new experience is different than the last. Only then can you recognize how quickly you are creating, shifting, and changing. The degree of difference from one moment to the next shows you how quickly you are creating new joyful experiences. Make this your definition of reality—and watch what happens!

Getting Real Exercise

Let's take a look at your current reality. By now, you may have completed the one-week challenge and have a better idea of how you feel most of the time. These regular checks with self are life-altering if you can put them into practice regularly. They assist you in stepping more fully into who you really are. Let's play again.

Part One:

Grab your journal, and let's uncover more of this inner you. Ask yourself these questions and answer them in the simplest way possible. Do your best not to get into much detail. Simply read the sentence and write whatever comes to mind. I've also given you a few suggestions to think about with each one.

What would I say is the reality of my current living situation? Am I living alone? Do I live in a house, an apartment, or a condo? Does anyone live with me, or do I live in someone's home? Is this the home my ex and I purchased together?

What would I say is the reality of my current work situation? Do I have a job I go to every day? Do I run my own business? Do I love what I am doing? Do I get along with the people in my work environment? Is this a career, or am I just passing through on my way to something better?

What would I say is the reality of my current social life? Do I go out with friends for fun? Do I have lots of friends or one or two close ones? Do I stay home a lot? Do I go out at all by myself? Do I have *any* friends?

You now have some very basic information regarding three areas of your life. *This is the way I see me right now.* There is nothing emotional about what you have recorded. You've simply made notes about some simple statements regarding how you perceive your life. This is your current reality.

Part Two:

Let's dig deeper to discover what emotions you have attached to each of these scenarios. Each of us has unique definitions of people, places, objects, situations, and events. You can't define anything without bringing your thoughts, emotions, and beliefs into the equation. It's human nature. Reality only scratches the surface, but personal experience is much deeper.

Answer this next group of questions while engaging your emotions. When you read each question, think about how you *feel* about these situations. Don't worry about how it used to be—or how you want it to be—just record how you feel about it right now.

How do I feel about my current living situation? Do I like it? Am I comfortable living here? Does it feel warm and cozy? How would I explain the spirit or vibe of this place? Does it feel as though I am in transition or as though I'm putting down roots? Is it lacking something? Does it feel like too much? Does it feel natural? Does it feel like mine or someone else's?

How do I feel about my current work situation? Do I wake up excited to go to work, or am I drained? Does this place bring me joy or make me feel overwhelmed? Are my coworkers wonderful, loving people or backstabbing workaholics? Does work feel like an escape or a prison? Is this place holding me back or am I excited about what I do here? Am I struggling in this area or do I love it?

How do I feel about my current social life? Am I comfortable with the friends I have? Do I feel as though I have lots of friends or hardly any at all? Am I lonely and wish I had more friends? Do I often stay home, wishing someone would call? When with friends, do we have laugh—or is my break-up the main topic of discussion? Am I jealous of my friends? Does my social life consist of family members or coworkers? Do I feel like my social life is exciting or boring?

You have now expanded emotionally on these areas. It is extremely difficult to define anything without engaging your thoughts, emotions, and beliefs. You now have a more detailed picture of how you feel about where you live, where you work or what you do, and your social life. In all life experiences, emotions are present. How you feel about what you perceive is unique to you—as it is for everyone else.

Your feelings are signals that provide guidance about whether something is true (feels good) or not true (feels nasty) for you. Most of us spend our lives trying to figure out why we made specific choices and chastise ourselves for screwing things up. We analyze the details and judge everything in order to draw conclusions. By simply paying attention to how something makes us feel, we can choose whether it is true for us or not. Other people's points of view never really matter. What does it mean when people define reality as "a state of things as they actually exist?" Who defines this? You do! Who else but you could define your reality?

Each of us defines our own reality and how it feels to us in a unique way. Everything, as seen through each person's eyes, could be, and is, defined differently. For example; your friends may have the impression that you have many friends and are a social butterfly, but you feel you have only a handful of close friends and many acquaintances.

In every moment, life evolves—and so does your definition of your reality. Your job is to decide whether the emotions you have attached to these definitions and the relationships you are developing are 100 percent true for you. If they don't feel light and right, you are not living your own life. You have bought into someone else's definition and adopted it as your own. We all like to believe that our own personal definitions are no different than anyone else's. Even though most will admit this isn't true, they often forget their uniqueness.

Recently, I was having a conversation with a friend about colors. I was sharing how I am much more out there with my color choices than she is.

With a concerned look, she replied, "Oh, don't get me wrong. I love color too—as long as it isn't ugly."

I instantly exploded with laughter. I couldn't help but wonder about her definition of ugly colors.

If I were to ask each of you what colors you found appealing to paint in your home, I would get a wide variety of colors. That is why paint stores exist. What you define as ugly could be beautiful to me. I adore color. If I chose to play with gold and brown as wall colors in my home, I would splash accents of teal, magenta, and ivory. I find deep mauve and brown with splashes of orange, lime green, and turquoise yummy. For many, my tasty palette would be considered too wild, bold, or even ugly.

My friend assumed that her definition of ugly was the same as mine. In her reality, she couldn't see it any other way. If I was to show her the colors I would choose to paint my home, she might say, "Why would you paint those colors? They're so bright! I wouldn't feel relaxed in my own home!" Describing something as "interesting" is also a nice way of saying it doesn't appeal to you. In my reality, bright colors make me feel warm, vibrant, and alive. It is as if everything is turned on!

Questioning your beliefs and definitions, which are how you make up your reality, grants you a powerful outlook. It helps you shed light on the areas where you feel trapped because your beliefs and definitions are not allowing you to see that there are unlimited possibilities. When you question what you view as your immediate reality—without challenging, fighting, or asking it to change—you surprise yourself with new, powerful possibilities.

When you challenge someone, their usual reaction is to go on guard and become defensive. You are asking them to change in order to make you happy. The things you have bought into as your beliefs and how you define your reality works the same way. By using curiosity, the outcome changes to one where others are willing to receive your ideas and question their own choices. They won't become defensive.

In the earlier exercise, you defined your reality as you see it with your eyes and shared your awareness of this. You then engaged your feelings and uncovered your relationship with it. Your beliefs and the definitions you give everything cause you to sum up every aspect of your current reality as good and right (light) or evil and wrong (heavy).

This language of thought is the contributing factor to your reality. If you are living with the mind-set that being single at this age is bad, wrong, difficult, a struggle, no fun, a drag, lonely, a headache, or nasty, you will get your wish. Your current reality is proof of it.

Your beliefs are all conditional; that is why you get stuck and can't move past them quickly and easily.

A friend of mine took her daughter on a holiday, and they stayed at a friend's cottage. The daughter spent her days sunning on the beach and reading books. In the evening, she joined her mother, and they enjoyed time with their hosts sightseeing, shopping, and eating in posh restaurants. What a fantastic time they had!

Upon leaving, the daughter expressed her thankfulness to the hosts for their hospitality.

About a week after they left, my friend said, "I am so proud of Marie. Do you know what she did? She asked me for Bob and Mary's e-mail address so she could send them a thank you e-mail for letting us stay at their cottage and for such a wonderful holiday. Isn't that thoughtful of her?"

Of course I agreed. It was very considerate of Marie to thank them once again.

She added, "It's nice to see she finally did this on her own, and I didn't have to tell her to do it. This is the first time she has taken the initiative to send a thank you e-mail on her own without my instructing her. I'm so proud!"

Are you kidding me? I could barely hold my tongue. I couldn't believe my friend was proud of her daughter only because she had completed a task she had been brainwashing her to do for years!

Let's take a look at this. Why was my friend proud? She was proud because her daughter followed what she defined as proper protocol for showing thanks. She has a belief that her daughter's actions are a direct reflection of her parenting and that others judge her as good or bad depending on the choices her daughter makes. This is a very conditional relationship. Can you see how she gives her power away? If her daughter chooses not to follow her guidance, she is the only one affected in a negative way. Her daughter held all her power in that situation.

Stresses can be related to beliefs and definitions. My friend's beliefs that her daughter's actions are a reflection of her parenting are not even hers. They are most likely her parents', and she simply adopted them as her own. Unfortunately, they are causing her to live a limited reality where precise conditions must be met in order for her to be happy.

Choosing to live from curiosity and question helps opens doors you never knew existed. This is what I want to encourage in you. When you have all the details about how anything new can appear, you lock it down—just as my friend did. You box yourself in with each detail. When your definition of showing thanks includes:

- saying how thankful and appreciative you are because you need to be acknowledged as thankful (you build a wall in front of you)
- upon arriving home, you send an e-mail, again expressing your thankfulness (you build a wall to your right)
- you expect confirmation of your appreciation (you build a wall behind you)
- you again share how thankful you are for their hospitality (you build a wall to your left)

Each expectation builds a wall, closing you in and disallowing any other possibility. When you play host and your guests don't follow your rules, you judge them. You need to bust through some of your beliefs to redefine definitions that are not working for you. Nothing is set in stone. Everything can be redefined, but it all starts with your words and thoughts.

Everyone defines what they see and experience differently. Beliefs are like possessions—stored facts in the mind from collected data. Forming a belief is one of the most basic and important features of the mind. But to believe something needn't involve actively reflecting on it. What we are told by other people, what the media tells us, is often adopted as our own truth. We accept other people's definitions of what reality is, without questioning it ourselves.

Reality is a temporary state. Everything constantly morphs and changes according to its environment. You are always moving forward, even when you feel stuck. Society and past circumstances do not dictate fact and truth. You can let it go. Being a single, forty-plus woman does not mean you have to follow any guidelines or labels society says exist for you. You get to beat your own drum! How cool is that?

Here is the final step of your exercise. Read what you've written and follow along with this short guided meditation.

Road of Unlimited Possibilities Meditation

Close your eyes and take a deep breath in through your nose. Hold for a count of three and let it out through your mouth with an "ah" sound. Repeat two more times. Now sit quietly for a moment, and feel your body breathing naturally. Feel the rise and fall of your chest and the beat of your heart.

Imagine you are walking down an open road in the middle of the country. It is a warm, summer afternoon. It's quiet. Everything is green and beautiful. Take a deep breath and feel it filling your lungs. Smell the fresh summer air. There is a bit of a breeze blowing. It's not too hot or too cold. Look around as you walk. It's peaceful here. What do you see? What does the landscape look like? What types of bushes, trees, and flowers are scattered about? Are there any houses nearby or in the distance? Quietly walk and look at your surroundings. Bring your attention back to the road. Is the road paved or is it a gravel road? Look far out in front of you. This is the Road of Unlimited Possibilities.

As you continue to joyfully walk down this road, focus your thoughts on a current situation you are struggling with. Ask, "I wonder what possibilities are available for me—now and in the future?" Don't draw any conclusions. Consider this question and continue walking down the road.

Up ahead, you can see that the road divides. Raise your arm in front of you and spread your fingers wide. The forks in the road ahead appear much like your hand. Continue walking joyfully until you reach the spot where the road divides.

You are now faced with the choice of which road to follow. Each road presents different experiences, and each includes hidden gems, synchronistic events, and more forks to choose from, but they all lead to a final destination associated to your question.

Take a moment to contemplate your expectations and whether they feel joyous or binding. Take a deep breath in and exhale as you release all fixed conclusions that are holding you stuck in regard to your question. Standing in this peaceful mind experience, cup your hands, making a bowl in front of you. Again, focusing on your questions, take a deep breath in, filling your lungs, and say, "What other possibilities are available for me, now and in my future?"

Exhale onto your hands as if you are blowing out a candle— and let the thought go. No conclusions. No decisions. No walls. Simply let it go, and shift your thoughts to curiosity and wonder.

Bring your attention back fully to the road. In front of each fork, you notice a rock with a word imprinted on it. You cannot read the word from where you are. You now must choose which fork to follow. Recall the current situation you are struggling with. Hold your arm out in front of you, point it toward one of the forks, and ask, "Will this road provide me with the most joyful experience regarding my situation?"

With your other hand, push down gently on your arm. If your arm drops slightly, the answer is no. If your arm stays strong, the answer is yes. Repeat this process in your mind for each fork—until you receive a yes.

Once you have made your choice, walk toward the stone in front of the fork you have chosen. Read the word on the rock, make a mental note of it, and continue down your new path, knowing all is well.

Bring your attention back to the present, and in your own time, open your eyes when you are ready. Write down the word from the rock and any details about how you felt during the meditation. The word on the rock will provide you guidance on this part of your life journey.

This meditation may bring up some interesting feelings for you. Its purpose is to help you move into a broader perspective and embrace the prospect of a bigger vision. Get into the feelings of something totally new, which makes you feel good and changes the old definition of you.

This is an easy exercise to play with if you are having difficulty with any situation. It shifts your energy and vibe into a more playful one of curiosity and wonder—where the magic of unlimited possibilities exists. We often get stuck thinking there are only one or two options for how any situation can unfold. In fact, there are an unlimited number of ways for circumstances to play out. Many aren't even on our radar, but we focus on one or two and create all sorts of unease within ourselves. They are most often the worst-case scenarios. What if an unlimited number of possibilities were available to us— and all we had to do to unlock them was shift into wonder?

Part Three:

Let's play with those questions again, but draw on wonder and curiosity this time. Ask yourself each question, and then do the road meditation again. If you let yourself go, you will start to release some of the crap you are struggling with and get an idea of the you emerging just below the surface. Once you have completed the above meditation for each question, record any findings in your journal.

What would be my ideal living situation? Would I most enjoy living out in the country, downtown, on a boat, in a loft apartment, or in a penthouse? How would living here make me feel? Would I reside in the country I currently live in or choose another one? Would I live alone or with someone? What else is possible in my ideal living environment?

What would be my ideal work environment? Would I work for a specific business or run my own? How much money do I make, and why would you not choose a higher income? What are my coworkers or employees like? Do I travel? Do I work from home? What else is possible in my ideal working environment?

What would be my ideal social life? Would I have lots of friends or only a few? Would I have a lover(s)? A boyfriend? A husband? A girlfriend? What types of activities would I do that are very different from the life I am living now? What are my friends like? Are they very different from the friends I currently have? What else is possible on my ideal social life?

Wasn't that fun? I hope you were able to let go of struggling with your old definition of reality and played with wonder and curiosity. Desire, desire, desire ... doesn't it feel great? Don't say, "This should change so I can feel good." Say, "This is what feels good to me."

Don't get all caught up in being one of my other least favorite words—selfish. I would like to throw that word in the trash forever! Couldn't you see the possibilities living in a new environment, working where you would most enjoy, and hanging with uplifting people? Do you know your mind does not know the difference between what you perceive as the real world and the dream world? By doing this exercise, you gave your mind a break, which releases tension and anxiety; discovered your desires, including how good they make you feel; engaged the creative side of your brain, which helps keep your brain running outside its normal thought processes; started to shift your beliefs by feeding yourself positive visions; and tapped into a forgotten part of you.

Isn't that fantastic? What a gem you have given yourself! You are so wonderful. You are actually gifting you this time to take a good look at what you are defining as your reality, and you are choosing whether it is what you really want. This meditation can be used to play with any definition you have bought into. Simply follow the process of asking similar questions and do the meditation.

Take a look at the definitions you have created and decide whether they are serving you in a positive way. The act of redefining and recreating yourself is the beginning of a fun journey. You will be guiding yourself toward the people, circumstances, places, and emotions that make you feel good. Nothing stays the same for very long. The more you can engage thoughts like the ones you created during this exercise, the sooner you will start to change some of your old thinking patterns.

Try it for a while. Quit taking life so seriously and have some fun with it. I'm an authority on taking things too seriously. Be a little more playful with your life. Take some of the visions you came up with and pretend they are part of your real day—now. Give yourself a little freedom to change.

Chapter Seven
WHO AM I?

Who are you? I bet you have no idea who you really are. I'll even take a gamble and suggest that most of you have lived the vast majority of your lives behind some sort of self-imposed mask. Masks, my friend, make it exceptionally challenging to remember your real desires.

We've played a little with the idea of creating a reality that includes some of your desires, but this is only the beginning. Did you know that most of your beliefs were adopted out of necessity instead of following your gut feelings? You've actually trained yourself to forget how to follow your intuition. Instead, you go to outside sources, such as girlfriends, close friends, therapists, or family members for answers. When you desire something you feel unworthy of having, you sum it up as being selfish or greedy. You compare yourself to friends, neighbors, coworkers, or family members to see how you measure up. You've been trained to keep a checklist of who has what—and you compare yourself to them.

Do you even know what excites you anymore? For years, weekends consisted of picking up groceries, running errands, cleaning the house, doing the laundry, or dropping on the sofa exhausted from an overstressed workweek. There are always chores to be done! My neighbor always says, "A woman's work is never done!"

I can't tell you how much I dislike that word. Chores: a small or odd job, a hard or unpleasant task. Yuck! Yuck! Yuck! What is this need to always be productive? If someone inquired about what you did for fun, would you even know?

This question stumped me when I was engaged in conversations with men on Internet dating sites. A guy checking you out wants to know what you enjoy doing with your free time. I had no idea how to respond. I was of the opinion that the types of activities I enjoyed would be thought of as boring. In truth, to some guys, I am a boring chick. I like to read books that make me question my beliefs and definitions (and write them too!). My favorite place to hang out is a bookstore. My laptop is an extended part of my body that permits me to write, take care of my websites, coach women, run telesummits, or listen to juicy motivational speakers. Other pastimes of mine include shopping, going to the movies, painting, doodling, chatting over tea, walking Chester Pug, and going out to dinner. For anyone who is an outdoorsy type, I'm a real drag!

How many times have you been asked how you spent your weekend and responded with all sorts of boring, productive stuff? If we allow ourselves to have some fun, we cram it in between these constructive weekend duties—way down on our list of priorities. Why is the fun stuff only allowed to take place on weekends? There are five full days ready for fun-ness in between, but we choose to wait until the weekend to try to cram it all in. Where are you in this whole mess? What masks have you designed for all of those special occasions? Why?

The Masquerade Party Never Dies

We all design and wear social masks. They are the images of ourselves we choose to present to the outside world. They are designed from your own interpretation of what we believe the public, or a specific environment, expects and considers acceptable. Do you act according to the situation? That's a mask. What are masks anyway?

The word persona means mask. The word *personality* comes from persona. Most often, masks are hiding places. They are the shields you use to guard your secret thoughts and feelings from those you don't trust. Each mask or persona is a compromise of who you truly are; they are designed to prevent the outside world from seeing your true magnificence. Most of you have no idea when you are even wearing a mask. They've been a part of you for so long that they feel like your favorite pair of shoes. It's not until you lose something that you realize it was there in the first place.

Unless you lose something and regain it, you never understand the beauty of having it.

Have you attended a masquerade party where you have worn a mask? Perhaps you attended a costume party as a child. While wearing the mask, you were hidden. Depending on how elaborate your costume was, you might have fooled people into wondering who you are. What's more important is how you feel when you are wearing the mask. What qualities does it give you that you don't feel you have? How does it keep the private you hidden? How does it protect and stand up for you?

Masks are the personas we create to help us handle different situations, circumstances, and people.

Let me share a few of my personal masks with you.

In the last few years of my marriage, I often slipped on my needy mask. I would slide it on approximately an hour before I expected my ex to arrive home. Its duty was to get his attention. I had grown tired of spending so many evenings alone and would do almost anything for the attention of my ex.

Around the time I expected him, I would climb into bed, peek out the bedroom window, and watch for him to pull in the driveway. Upon his arrival, I would slip on my needy mask and wait for him to come looking for me. I cannot express how much I simply desired that he find me. Let me clarify that I did not do this intentionally. Sometimes you slip masks on so silently that you don't even realize you've done so. Masks are generally created out of a yearning for something. In my case, I desired my ex's attention.

The ugly part of this story was that when he did arrive home, he rarely came looking for me. I would stay in the bed, wishing he would be concerned of my whereabouts. Instead, I heard him clunking around in the kitchen searching for food. I wanted so much for him to come snuggle beside me, and I hoped for any display of love from him. My mask failed me, but I continued to wear it—and hope.

Masks aren't a true projection of who you allow yourself to be. You design masks with the qualities and characteristics you believe you require in order to better handle a specific situation, function in a particular environment, or deal with specific people or social settings. They help you play the chameleon and allow you to blend in. They are a way of giving yourself permission to play with qualities you normally don't call on. A mask can allow your inner bitch to come out to play or your pain and suffering to come to the surface. Usually you would not share these qualities because you feel they are unacceptable.

One of my oldest masks is the one I wore to fit in at work. This mask hid the loving, caring, spiritual me. It is the most cruel, unfeeling mask I have ever designed. As I became more conscious of how much I liked who I was, I could sense the exact moments when I slipped it on.

Every time I entered that toxic work environment, I said, "Catherine, this is not who you really are, but it will help you fit in and get you through another day here." I would slip it on and take my place in the ranks as a wolf. Although it was the most uncomfortable mask I have ever worn—and I choose never to wear it again—wearing it was the only way I could function as a manager at this company. I referred to it as my wolf mask, allowing me to be the sheep in wolf's clothing. Its scrutinizing, judging eyes hid all loving expression and emotion. It was on attack at all times, doing its job to conceal the real me from the people I worked with and providing me a false sense of security.

Near the end of my time working in that setting, wearing it became difficult. From time to time, I felt compelled to slip it off and reveal bits of who I really was to my peers. Without the mask, I was able to see my peers clearly—through eyes of love and compassion. I noticed the more I gave myself permission to allow the real me to shine through, the more my peers would share parts of their true selves as well. Sadly, I wasn't comfortable exposing me for very long because wolves lurked around every corner, ready to pounce.

I've done my share of self-exploration over the past fifteen years, and I have been fortunate to identify many of my own masks. I sincerely believe the truth will set you free. My *confidence* mask led others to believe I was extremely confident. My *sheep-in-wolf's-clothing* mask allowed me to fit into the ranks of hard-hearted managers, protecting my personal beliefs and desires. My *victim/unloved-wife* mask tried to garner attention from my ex. My *big-shoulders* mask was for handling tough emotional situations, such as my father's death.

They were exaggerated versions of me. Can you identify any of yours? Take a moment to sit quietly and think about it. What masks have you designed? What purpose do they serve? Do you have masks you wear when you encounter specific people? Is there someone in your life you struggle around? Is there somebody who pushes your buttons? If so, what mask do you wear in their presence?

For most of my life, I found it difficult to share myself with others. That's how masks are designed in the first place. You design them when you need to call on a character trait you believe you do not have. They are the personas you create to deal with difficult situations, circumstances, people, and places.

I've seen people wear masks to appear to be happy-go-lucky when they are truly miserable and pumping themselves full of antidepressants. I've watched masks trick others into believing they are lovable and spiritual when they struggle with spirituality and spend most of their energy manipulating people in order to feel better about themselves. Some people wear masks to control others, using them to ensure everyone they love is kept safe out of a fear of losing them. You might even design a mask to fit in with a specific group of people. You could design a mask to assist you in releasing stress. Perhaps you have even designed one that stands up for you—if normally you wouldn't have a voice.

If you want to remember who you are and embrace everything you are passionate about, detecting and exposing your masks will be a valuable process. I have found the best way to reveal them is to become aware of the times when you aren't wearing them.

When I'm walking Chester Pug, I'm not wearing a mask. It's 100 percent me, walking joyfully and taking in the wonders of the world while Chester Pug prances along happily. I'm simply walking, breathing in the fresh air, and enjoying how quiet it is. There's no mask there.

While writing, I don't wear a mask. When I write, I get into the flow of my thoughts. In my head, I am talking to a large group. I am simply me, speaking from my inner knowing. I like to express my true feelings, and writing is a fantastic way to do this.

Driving is another time I know I'm not wearing a mask. Driving is often used as a form of release, referred to as road rage. For some, driving provides an outlet to push through everyone around them. Does this sound like something you do? This mask allows the wearer to be a complete idiot behind a steering wheel. In revealing this mask and taking it off, I now drive in comfort and joy. Instead of doing the mad drive to work, cursing at people who are not driving fast enough or flipping the bird to anyone who cuts me off, I enjoy my surroundings.

I continue to identify these limiting masks and open my eyes to what is really around me. A calmer me has emerged. Masks do a good job of blinding us from the truth. This is something you will embrace as you stop worrying about what everyone else is up to—and start paying attention to your own needs and desires. Many would call this being selfish. I like to think I am sharing my authentic self with others. In doing so, I am an example of how to live in a more genuine way.

Can you identify a time when you don't wear a mask? Get out your trusty journal, open it to a fresh page, and write: I don't wear a mask when … and fill in the blanks.

How about in the shower? Have you ever noticed when you are taking your morning shower that your mind is often streaming all kinds of crap? I call this "yesterday's mask." It conjures up all sorts of thoughts and emotions from yesterday's experiences, and it keeps a negative ball rolling. What a horrible way to begin your day! Try this exercise during your next morning shower.

> Step in the shower stall, and with your back to the water, close your eyes. Take three deep breaths into your belly and release each one as slowly as possible. The trick is to connect with your senses. Really connect! Bring your attention to your skin and your nose. Now, step back into the hot water slowly. Submit entirely to your senses. Get out of your head and connect with your body. Feel the hot water caressing your neck and shoulders. Feel it running down over your skin, on your legs and feet. Begin to slowly wash your body. Smell the scent of the soap and how wonderful it feels to scrub your body. Listen to the sound of the water. Take off yesterday's mask—and soak in some bubbles!

I choose to consciously use this time to think about things that bring me joy, which you can incorporate into your shower as well. Simply begin your shower with one amazing thought—and hold on to it during your whole shower time. I don't wear any masks in the shower.

You may notice one of the places you don't wear a mask is with your peeps. Even if you only have one good friend, what's different about the way you act and feel when you are with these people that doesn't require you to put on a mask? I'm New Age—and so are most of my friends. We seek universal truth. This usually includes elements of older spiritual traditions combined with science. We draw on intuition and personal desires when sharing with each other. We all know that when we tend to ourselves, humanity also benefits.

My friends are amazing spiritual gods and goddesses who are filled with knowledge and love. They are open to new information and experiences of the mind, body, and spirit. This is one of the reasons I am no longer married. My ex was under the assumption I had joined some kind of cult. Little did he know I was learning how to be an invitation to more expansive experiences in my life.

I have a very eclectic group of friends. My shaman friend thrives on standing up for issues involving the rights of others. I enjoy my nature enthusiast friend who wants to heal the planet. She also uses her powerful creative side to express her true self. I adore my crafty friend who can take anything from an idea, a thought, a painting, or actual clay—and sculpt it into abundance. I have friends who are incredibly balanced and love to make spaces unique and inviting. Others are entrepreneurs who run their own businesses. Some are energy healers who communicate with spirits. I am truly blessed to be surrounded by a variety of lovely souls who continually inspire me. When I am with these women, I wear no masks. Who can you be with who doesn't require you to wear a mask?

My favorite cousin is amazing. I used to wear a mask around her, but I don't even remember what the mask was. Maybe it was the stupid-little-cousin mask. When I was younger, I always felt I was in her shadow, but suddenly we connected. She showed interest in my world, which opened a door to a different way of being with each other. I was finally able to reveal my true self to her. Do you have certain family members you enjoy being with where you are simply yourself?

Is there an activity you enjoy participating in where time slips away quickly? Jogging, biking, photography, painting and writing are all good examples. These will be times that the masks are in the closet!

Are you having difficulty identifying when exactly you don't wear a mask? Try taking the opposite approach and identify the times when you do wear one. It's important to understand how you feel when you are not wearing a mask. Being who you really are doesn't feel uptight or restricting in any way. It just feels good.

Can you imagine what it would feel like to wear a real mask on your face all day? Imagine getting up in the morning, washing your face, putting on your makeup, doing your hair, getting dressed, and slipping on a mask before you leave home. Before that moment, you were relaxed. As soon as you popped on that mask, you identified with a different set of character traits. Your breathing immediately switched from long, deep, relaxed breaths to short, choppy ones—and your body tenses. Slipping on a mask instantly changes how you perceive yourself and cuts you off from who you really are. That's why wearing one feels so terrible. Unfortunately, we continue to slip them on. It is like a defense system or building a wall of protection that cuts us off from our divine selves.

Close your eyes and picture yourself walking out your front door, leaving the comfort of your home. If your home is not a happy place for you, choose a place where you feel comfortable. Get in touch with how it feels to be comfortable with who you are in that moment. Continue visualizing this comfort zone until you get to a place where you believe you need to hide yourself. For some of you, your workplace is your sanctuary. If your home life is stressing you out, you may wake up with a mask already on!

At some point in this short visualization, picture yourself reaching up and covering your face as you place a mask over it. What does it feel like? Does it feel thick, heavy, uncomfortable, stuffy, unnatural, and phony? Remember that the moment you slip it on, you take on a quality you believe supports you in that moment. It could be:

- *Work Bi*ch Mask*—who uses fear as a manipulation tool because you have a belief that fear makes people work harder and faster.
- *Know-It-All Mask*—who always has an answer because, goodness knows, you're not stupid!
- *I-Have-It-All Mask*—who doesn't talk to anyone who isn't making six figures or has a university degree because they're nobodies.
- *My-Way-Is-Best Mask*—who enjoys showing everyone how to do everything the right way because they are all so incompetent.
- *Nothing-Good-Ever-Happens-to-Me Mask*—who plays the victim so everyone will think she's worthy when things happen to turn out in her favor.
- *Party Girl Mask*—who acts that way because everyone likes a girl who is the life of the party.
- *I'm Invisible Mask*—who does her best to stay out of harm's way and remain unnoticed.

Masks cover the qualities you are ignoring within yourself. These are characteristics you prefer not to support and would be ashamed to display. At some point in your life, you came to a conclusion that having these qualities got you something. This is always attributable to an example provided by someone else. It's no wonder that masks don't feel natural when you first design them. They aren't yours to begin with, and they are designed to hide the real you from the world. They are proof of a choice you made to cut a piece of yourself off in order to fit someone else's definition of what is acceptable. This quality the mask gives you is not one you believe is really a part of you.

Who we are is something most of us keep very close. We all have our reasons. Most of us can't imagine our beliefs changing significantly at any age, but we can quickly identify that our preferences have changed when we compare who we believe we are today with who we believe we were ten years ago. The fact is, most of us are afraid to share our private selves. We don't believe we are acceptable. Maybe we are afraid of being hurt or abandoned, and we shield ourselves with a durable coat of detachment, making us unavailable.

Masks give us permission to overcompensate for specific qualities by overdramatizing others. For example, we may play the victim role in order to fully support those who are victimized. This comes from the belief that we must be what we fight for. We might lavish others with attention and adoration to make them feel important and loved if we do not feel lovable. This is how masks are designed.

There are trillions of reasons why people create masks, but it's important to understand how each mask cuts off a piece of you that you regard as unacceptable and enables you to function in a reality you believe exists.

In my teens, I made a choice to hide my emotions. I came to the conclusion that being seen as emotional made me an easy target. My father and I did not get along well. Unfortunately, many young girls feel they do not meet the expectations of their fathers. My father was a sickly man who lived with a constant fear of dying. His heart disease and physical pain caused him to become disconnected from the loving man he really was. This pain and fear was hard for him to conceal. When in the presence of strangers, friends, or acquaintances, he would slip on his I-am-lovable mask, convincing all he was in the best of spirits. It worked extremely well because, from what I could see, everyone loved my father.

However, when not outside chatting to the neighbors, the mask came off. The more I watched him lovingly interact with others, the farther away I pushed myself from him. I was angry that I never got to interact with the I-am-lovable father. Instead, his family got the full outpouring of his pain and fear. I didn't know that my father actually removed all his masks in his family's presence and allowed his true vulnerable state of mind to be seen. However, in my teenage eyes, there was no praise for a job well done. Nothing I did ever seemed good enough. One day I designed a "Whatever! You can't hurt me!" mask, and that was it.

That was the point in my life where I started to bury my emotions. Appearing emotionally cold felt better than feeling unimportant and unloved. It seemed easier to pretend I didn't care than to worry about the day my father would pass away. That's how quickly it happens—one thought and that mask was created! From that day forward, I chose to hide the loving, vivacious, compassionate, and emotional me; I only shared my tough outer shell.

We live in an environment where limitation has been taught for generations. The masks we create and wear always serve us in some way. As a result of an experience from the past, you believe that certain qualities are desirable. Someone in your life was an example of how having a certain quality was a benefit, or a hindrance, and you chose to support it in your personality. For example, you didn't know that being likable could show up in any other way besides the way it was presented to you at a young, impressionable age. So you copied this mask from someone else and slipped it on whenever it served you. Now it is how you define being likable. This mask is actually not a true representation of who you are. It is a tool you choose to support or not support in different situations.

You can't hide these parts of who you are forever. We all have certain qualities that are stronger than others. There are also those we have decided are unacceptable; we tell ourselves we are nothing like that and design a mask to prove otherwise. Do you let someone else decide what qualities and characteristics are acceptable for you?

Let's play some more and see if you can reveal the secrets of one of your masks. You may recognize periods when you are wearing one without understanding the purpose of the mask. Go ahead and recall a time when you wore a mask. Close your eyes and embody the feeling this mask provides. Do you have a difficult time without it? You've given this mask some amazing powers. Unfortunately, this means you've given some of your power away and allowed the mask to be your hiding place. What or who are you hiding from? What don't you want to reveal about yourself and why? What beliefs are you harboring that aren't serving you?

The mask I wore when I climbed into bed waiting for my ex to arrive home was a reflection of my pain and loneliness.

I slipped the victim mask on to get attention. Because I am not good at expressing pain to anyone, this mask helped me connected with the wounded part of me, and it allowed me to express my feelings of abandonment. Acting in this way is something I have suppressed in the past as a result of an old belief I adopted: *Showing emotion is a sign of weakness.*

I have many examples stored away in my subconscious, and my ego enjoys reminding me of them. Abandonment is a fear I swallowed to hold back tears, which I was taught was another sign of weakness. I literally swallowed whenever I felt the urge to cry. I cut off my body's natural way of releasing stress and tension. Why would anyone do that? The answer is always right there behind the mask. All you have to do is take it off and have the guts to ask.

Do you interpret your painful past experiences as being insignificant compared to the tragedies of others? You don't talk about your problems or cry; you just keep it all to yourself. You think that what you are going through is nothing compared to the pain and suffering that others live with, and you choose not to share it with anyone. The consequences of such actions are overwhelmingly destructive.

I've talked a lot about barfing because it's what most of us do. Many women have designed masks so thick that it would take a hammer and chisel to chip them away to reveal the blubbering woman below the surface. Is it an impossible task? Of course not! It just takes the desire to do so. These masks were designed at a very early age, and they are all about self-worth and feeling insignificant. Lots of hiding is going on here. If this sounds like you, keep working through the processes in this book.

Most of us wouldn't dare ask ourselves these questions. What we don't know can't hurt us, correct? Good one! I've used it myself. I hope you discover that in order to find who you really are, you can't continue to ignore how you feel about everything and all of your amazing talents and gifts. Right now you have the most scrumptious opportunity to simply be you. Now is the time to receive this opportunity and do what you really enjoy without the need for anyone's permission. You can read what you want, eat the food you love without having to please anyone else, decorate with your own feminine flair (making you feel sexy and alive), sing, dress how you choose, watch what you want, and even choose to be alone and feel sorry for yourself—or go out with friends and celebrate where you are in your life right now. Most importantly, discover that now is the most perfect place for you to be. To do this, you will have to take off some masks, understand the purpose they served, and start functioning without them.

A Mask Revealed

It is time to play some more. Close your eyes and recall one of your masks. Get into the groove of how it makes you feel when you are wearing it. Who are you when you have attached yourself to it? Reach up and remove it. Set it down in front of you and ask yourself the questions below. Take the time to sit quietly and get ready to receive the information from your inner knowing; it may show up as pictures, words, past memories, or gut feelings. Record your findings in your journal.

What Mask I Am Wearing?

Give your mask a name. Here are a few ideas if you are stuck:

- *I can do it all*
- *I know the right way to do everything*
- *I'm the boss who everyone fears*
- *wolf in sheep's clothing*—I am truly judging, critical, and backstabbing, but I cover this all up to fit in with my peers

by pretending to be what I think they define as supporting and loving

- *sheep in wolf's clothing*—I am truly loving and supporting of those around me, but I hide these aspects by being cruel and judging to fit into a specific environment or group of people
- *I know a lot, and everyone needs to hear what I have to say*
- *if I laugh loud and make jokes, everyone will think I am just fine*
- *I'm a single mom so I am helpless*
- *everyone needs to believe what I believe*
- *party girl who everyone loves*
- *hip cougar mama*
- *nothing ever gets under my skin*
- *I don't rock the boat and go along with what others say*
- *victim*—I feel like everyone is out to get me
- *I can't make my own decisions*—If someone else makes them, I can blame them and not take ownership for making stupid decisions

How Does This Mask Serve Me?

Why are you wearing this silly thing anyway? What is it doing for you? Uncover why and how this mask serves you. My victim mask gave me the power to release an overdramatized version of how I was really feeling. I thought by being vulnerable, my ex would feel sorry for me, reach out, and actually provide physical contact.

What Beliefs Have You Attached to This Mask?

Beliefs are always attached to masks. "I am a single mom, so I am helpless" could have certain beliefs attached to it like. *I'm supposed to be married and have a man in my life to take care of me. Single moms don't have anyone to help them.* If your mother was a single mom, you might have learned this by example.

"If I laugh loud enough, everyone will think I am just fine" could have core beliefs too. *People who laugh are always happy. No one ever thinks anything is wrong with people who are always laughing, so I can keep my depression or addiction a secret. It's always the quiet ones you have to worry about. People really don't give a hoot about anyone else's problems. If you can laugh loudly and make jokes, everyone sees you as a confident person.*

Are These Beliefs True or Even Mine?

Most of your beliefs are not even your own; how can you be sure they are true for you if you have never even questioned them? They are not based on any deep thought or questioning. You simply accepted them as truths.

Entertain the idea that your beliefs are the cause of all the events in your life. If you changed your beliefs to ones that served you, your outside experiences would begin to reflect these new ideas. Your current beliefs are actually some of your biggest limitations. Do you really believe when someone smiles and laughs that they don't have any worries? Why? Who says so? Who led you to believe this? How do you know what you don't know? How does this belief serve you? Is everything really more difficult without a partner? Isn't life sometimes cloudier when you have a partner? You both have different points of views and priorities. Do you assume your partner is thinking the same things as you? That's what gets us into trouble in the first place! How does this belief serve you?

It doesn't matter whether or not your beliefs are actually true. What does matter is whether you are moving away from or toward the things you desire.

Do I Feel Good When I Am Wearing This Mask?

How does the mask make you feel when you know you are wearing it? Are you proud to wear it? If it doesn't feel good, it is not good. Get rid of it (I know this is easier said than done). If the mask makes you feel empowered in some way, ask what the mask provides that you are missing.

Fighter-You Always Gets You What You Deserve

Imagine yourself sitting at your kitchen table. Now conjure up another you sitting to your left. We're going to call this second version of you fighter-you. Her duty is to get you everything you know you deserve—but are too ashamed to go after out of a fear of being judged. Fighter-you knows she can work her magic and obtain anything you want because she has a grand purpose in your life.

Now imagine a huge pile of money on the table and a group of people who appear to be extremely poor sitting in the chairs across from you. The money is up for grabs to whoever takes it first.

As you salivate looking at the huge pile of money, understand that everyone desires happiness. We all have a desire to be released from what we perceive as suffering—no matter how we define it. Everyone at the table sees this huge pile of money and begins to envision all they could accomplish from having it. No matter who gets the money, there is no right or wrong about it. Suddenly, fighter-you jumps up and snatches every cent! She worked her magic and got just what you wanted.

How do you feel about this? Are you okay with how fighter-you handled this situation? Are you feeling good or terrible? If the people who appeared to be poor had grabbed all the hooch, how would you be feeling? Would you feel robbed of the opportunity to have an easier, more enjoyable life? Are you not as worthy of having money? How do you know their situation is any more deserving than yours? Who decides who is deserving—and who isn't?

This example is designed to push your buttons. Even though these masks feel terrible, they also feed a deep desire. Fighter-you is off creating wonderful experiences with that money and enjoying life. How do you feel right now? How much are you allowing the fear of judgment make you feel bad about fighter-you's actions? In what ways could this scenario have played out so you would feel good without the mask? There is no right or wrong answer to this question.

Masks serve a purpose, but they are not always comfortable. They can cause you to act in ways you may not be proud of. They sometimes do or say things you regret. What if you could take the qualities of the mask, which are already characteristics hidden within you, and use them in ways to make you feel good?

Part of getting rid of the need for masks means having to embrace the idea that the qualities they provide are already a part of you. When you welcome the idea that all characteristics and qualities are part of that which you are, you are more able to live fully from your truth. Ask if there is a way to incorporate some of the aspects of this mask into who you really are now. After all, we do have access to all human characteristics.

How Can I Get Rid of the Mask?

A little at a time. Reveal the first one, and then gradually test taking off more of them and exposing the real you to the world—and see what happens.

Getting rid of masks can be an interesting process and a bit of a challenge. We are used to wearing them to help us function in certain environments, and when we try to get rid of them, we often replace them with ones that have the exact opposite traits, thinking this will counteract them.

Let's say you are an office manager in an overstressed workplace who has become accustomed to wearing The boss mask. Let's say you define this mask in this way:

- I am the leader of a team and have the final say in all decisions—whether my employees agree with me or not.
- I expect my employees to communicate with me with the utmost of respect at all times—even if they disagree with my decisions.
- As the boss, I work endless overtime, believing this proves my dedication. I expect my employees to do the same—or I view them as not being team players.
- I pretend not to care if anyone likes me—as long as they fear and respect me.
- Although I do want my employees to think outside of the box and come up with new and adventurous ideas, I don't allow them to make suggestions to anyone besides me.
- I am in full control of my team.

This is a complex, egotistical, controlling mask. The poor wearer is actually so disconnected from who they really are that they have a need to control others in order to feel better about themselves. This mask fits the wearer like a glove. They are so used to wearing it that they have no idea how to function in this position without it. They may not be willing to remove it.

In this situation, when we attempt to remove the mask, we often replace it with one that has the opposite qualities. In this example, you may inherently exchange The boss mask for the loving-boss mask. Doing so would inevitably head you into even deeper water because it's very likely that no one is going to take you seriously.

The boss mask has trained people to work out of fear of you, under your thumb, to act as robots following your every order. As the wearer of this mask, you may not be aware of the effect it has created. Have you invented it as a result of your own insecurities and lack of self-confidence? Control is the key factor. Is your past dotted with experiences and people who have made you feel incompetent and small? Wearing this mask gives you permission to show the world that you are a powerful person. You have the right idea, but your definition of a powerful person is rather disempowering.

While wearing this mask, you are not allowing your employees to use 100 percent of their skills and talents. Creative ideas do not flow from fear. If you suddenly do a switcheroo and paste on the loving-boss mask, no one is going to take you seriously. The story of the scorpion and the frog comes to mind.

The Scorpion and the Frog

One day, a scorpion looked around at the mountain where he lived and decided he wanted a change. So he set out on a journey through the forests and hills. He climbed over rocks and under vines and continued until he reached a river.

The river was wide and swift, and the scorpion stopped to reconsider the situation. He couldn't see any way across. So he ran upriver and then checked downriver, all the while thinking he might have to turn back.

Suddenly, he saw a frog sitting in the rushes by the bank of the stream on the other side of the river. He decided to ask the frog for help getting across the stream.

"Hello, Mr. Frog!" called the scorpion across the water. "Would you be so kind as to give me a ride on your back across the river?"

"Well now, Mr. Scorpion! How do I know if I try to help you, you won't try to kill me?" asked the frog hesitantly.

"Because," the scorpion replied, "if I try to kill you, then I would die too, for you see I cannot swim!"

Now this seemed to make sense to the frog, but he asked, "What about when I get close to the bank? You could still try to kill me and get back to the shore!"

"This is true," agreed the scorpion. "But then I wouldn't be able to get to the other side of the river!"

"All right then ... how do I know you won't just wait till we get to the other side and then kill me?" said the frog.

"Ah," crooned the scorpion. "Because you see, once you've taken me to the other side of this river, I will be so grateful for your help that it would hardly be fair to reward you with death, now would it?"

So the frog agreed to take the scorpion across the river. He swam over to the bank and settled himself near the mud to pick up his passenger. The scorpion crawled onto the frog's back, his sharp claws prickling into the frog's soft skin, and the frog slid into the river. The muddy water swirled around them, but the frog stayed near the surface so the scorpion would not drown. He kicked strongly through the first half of the stream, his flippers paddling wildly against the current.

Halfway across the river, the frog suddenly felt a sharp sting in his back; out of the corner of his eye, he saw the scorpion remove his stinger from the frog's back. A deadening numbness began to creep into his limbs.

"You fool!" croaked the frog, "Now we shall both die! Why on earth did you do that?"

The scorpion shrugged and did a little jig on the drowning frog's back.

"I could not help myself. It is my nature."

The frog should have paid closer attention to his intuition. This is how your employees will feel if you make such a drastic change. The boss mask already has them defensive, and they will not be as easily fooled as the frog was. What you have worked so hard to instill in your employees will not be so easily undone. Wearing a sugarcoated mask will only put them on alert.

What do you do? Start with the questions I've provided. You want to get an idea of why you wear this hideous mask in the first place. Unveil what silly, old beliefs you have attached to it. Ask if these beliefs are even yours. Controlling masks never work in the wearer's favor—even if we think they do. I've watched these types of masks come back to bite the wearer in the butt so many times in the last twenty-three years that I could write another book about those stories alone!

You have to be willing to question your own beliefs instead of defending them. When you feel the need to defend your beliefs, you are also in a place of not feeling very good. That negative, defensive feeling is not going to help you redeFIND your life in a new, positive, loving way.

You can always tell when a belief is not really true for you because you feel the need to defend it. If you truly believe in something and someone challenges it (telling you it's wrong or stupid), you don't care. There's no energy surrounding it. You don't suddenly feel charged up and want to snap their heads off. You are aware that someone else has a different opinion or viewpoint. When you know something is absolutely true for you, you just know. Nothing anyone can say pushes your buttons.

Open your journal to a fresh page and start defining as many of the masks you have designed as possible. Begin by picking a mask that isn't such a big deal to you. One as dominant as the boss mask may a bit of a challenge to begin with. It's been given a lot of power. Pick one that doesn't feel so overwhelming. Give yourself some time each day to ask yourself the suggested questions. Don't rush. There are no time frames for completing this. Take your time and break one mask down at a time.

Passions, purpose, and joy are behind those masks. When you reveal them, good stuff will start to happen. Step into the experience of being a seasoned, forty-plus woman without wearing any masks.

Chapter Eight
YOU'VE GOT THE POWER

Now that we've begun to unravel some of the mystery around masks, let's look at how they take your power away—and what this phrase really means. When I was a child, I remember hearing people using the expression, *You are giving away your power.* I thought, *What are these hippie people talking about?*

As someone who loves to get to the bottom of things, I've come to learn this secret hippie language and understand what these airy, flowery people were trying to say to all of the overwhelmed, overstressed overachievers.

A brilliant student of one of my Living the Law of Attraction classes summed it up perfectly. She offered to share her interpretation of this phrase she once struggled to understand. She said, "Imagine you are wearing a turquoise shawl and someone says, 'I hate turquoise! I never wear that color! It's so bold! It almost looks like a fake color if you ask me!' Suddenly you feel uncomfortable and take the shawl off. Even if you decide not to take it off, you feel awful because wearing it made you happy. And now that you've taken this comment personally, you have shifted into judgment of yourself.

The reason you feel so terrible is because you've given someone else the power to decide what makes you feel good. You've allowed another person to make a choice for you, and you made a conscious choice to go along with it. Now you won't feel good wearing the shawl unless this person gives you permission to do so. You have given your power to them."

What a smart woman she is! She understood that when you do something to please someone else—and feel unhappy—you give your power away. Pretty simple, wouldn't you agree? There is now a condition to your happiness. You will never feel comfortable wearing the shawl in the presence of this person. Another person's pleasure should never come at the expense of your own. If this person were to suddenly leave the room, you might be brave enough to put the shawl back on, taking back some of your power in their absence. However, I bet you will never wear turquoise around this person again without worrying about them chastising you for doing so.

When you wear masks, you give your power to the mask. This could be interpreted as giving yourself more power because you have given the mask a trait you feel you are lacking—one you feel you need to deal with a specific situation or person. When I put on my sheep-in-wolf's-clothing mask, I hid my true self from everyone. I let the wolf do all my dirty work and felt good knowing that this is not who I really am. Plus, wearing it allowed me to put the blame on someone else—instead of myself. I did not feel safe sharing the private me in a place where I had the impression others would attack at a moment's notice. Instead of being myself, I chose to put on this mask to feel safe. I gave my power away to a mask. It felt suffocating. I am not a sheep in wolf's clothing any more than I am a sheep or a wolf. I am an artist, a writer, a people watcher, a highly intuitive energy reader, a light worker, an animal lover, a storyteller, a teacher, a lover of friends, an analyzer, a computer junky, and so much more.

How can you be a contribution to the world while hiding your magnificence? What abilities and talents are you keeping locked away, afraid they will be taken from you? What capacity and power are you holding down? Plugging into everyone else and giving them your power will eventually catch up with you. You can only give away so much of yourself before the tables begin to turn.

I am surrounded by friends who have accepted and play with the knowledge that we are the creators of our own life experiences. Because my peeps and I believe our only purpose on this planet is to seek joy, awareness of our emotions is amplified. I have learned—and share with those I attract into my life—that awareness of your feelings is the key to attracting everything that will make you happy. When you are aware of how you feel at all times and make conscious choices to choose what feels true to you, you are no longer giving away your power.

Imagine if a coworker walked up to you and said, "Some people view you as not being a team player. Everyone here works long hours—except you. We are all here from as early as seven to as late as eight. You work only the hours you have to." Most would immediately and without thinking hand their power over to this person, apologize, and feel fear bubbling up inside. Then they would walk away feeling frustrated with the objective of sharing this experience with anyone who would listen. They would feel scared, anxious, and angry.

What if you could approach this situation from the viewpoint of curiosity instead of fear? Curiosity shifts you into question and out of a defensive stance. Imagine if you could stop time when these words were being spoken. As you listened to this person barf (project their fears and negativity onto you), you could ask yourself questions. *I wonder how wanting to make me feel bad serves them in their own search for happiness? How can I contribute to myself by simply knowing this is just a point of view they have—without taking it personally?* It's an interesting twist to how we normally process experiences, isn't it? If all kinds of conclusions are mingling in your mind right now, do your best not to be harsh or judging of yourself, and remain curious.

Finding answers never gets you anywhere. They just stop you from receiving possibilities you don't know exist. Don't try to decide what is right or wrong. Maybe this person hates having to work long hours in order to impress *their* boss—and does so because they are fearful of losing their job. Was the same message delivered to them not so long ago, and they are angry for giving away their power? The fact that you are getting away with something that they weren't able to might be getting under their skin. After all, shouldn't we all be miserable together? Did you ever stop to think this person might feel better about their own predicament, knowing you felt insecure about yours? I know this sounds immature, but people are only motivated to do what makes them feel good.

When we react to situations, we always choose what feels best for us emotionally.

It may not be the best choice, invite new possibilities, or even feel wonderful, but we always choose what we believe feels best for us emotionally. Sometimes we make painful choices instead of choosing an entirely new option because we are more fearful of making a choice when we have no idea of the outcome. What we know, although it is painful, is familiar. Choosing something we don't have any history or proof of (the unknown) sends us into panic.

I stayed in the relationship with my ex because it was familiar. I was afraid to venture out and look for something new. What if it was worse? What if I couldn't succeed on my own? I was terrified of making the wrong decision. I chose to continue to stay in an unhappy, familiar relationship instead of making a leap of faith.

My friend used to laugh and say, "Catherine, how bad are you going to make this situation before you can't take it any longer?"

I'm not suggesting that you disobey anyone in order to keep your power. If you look at the situation from the viewpoint of curiosity and love, you will always see it for what it really is—and you will have a better chance of not taking those comments so personally.

What is really happening is that you are picking up on someone else's emotions as if they are yours. This person storms into your space, throwing around angry energy, accusations, and feelings of being attacked—and you grab on to those emotions as if they are yours. When you take things personally, you give away your power. When you feel rotten and scared, you hand over your power. When you feel disempowered, you hand over your power. When you feel vengeful and angry, you hand over your power. When you feel calm, secure, energized, and joyful, you are in control of your power.

That's what the hippies were trying to tell us while they were dancing around all happy and free. Someone who is yelling at you has their own thing going on. What may appear to be an attack on you is really an attack on them. Someone yelling at you to complete a task in a specific way that makes them happy (the I'm-right-and-you-are-wrong syndrome) is really giving you their power. They are the one flustered and upset. Their desire to get a task completed in a certain way is in your hands. You have all the power!

In the two weeks before I left that toxic work environment, I was completing a project. The printer informed my boss that he was having problems downloading our files. My boss instructed me to burn all of the files that were uploaded onto the server to a CD. I burned all the files I had uploaded and proudly and promptly gave him the disc. Upon receiving it, he smiled oddly and asked again if everything on the server was on the disc. To my recollection, everything I had uploaded was there. He sent the disk to the printer.

Within an hour, I was abruptly called into his office. He said, "Catherine, did you burn *all* the files on the server onto that CD?"

I explained I had burned all the files I had uploaded onto the CD.

"I told you to put *everything* on the server onto a disk! That included all the files I had uploaded as well, and you did *not* follow my directions!"

In that instant, I handed him my power. I felt incompetent. I also understood what that sly smile was all about. He had set me up to fail. Our working relationship had never been promising, and now he had proof that made me appear to be a fool. I had fallen into the scorpion's trap. I felt rotten because I had been in control of all outgoing projects for years. I gave my power to him and walked away deflated. When he confronted me again later about my poor listening skills, I gave even more of my power away by moving into a defensive position, justifying my actions.

I could have kept my power by not taking it personally and getting defensive. I knew something was wrong about this whole situation. I knew this man wanted control. I watched as he created similar scenarios with other employees, and I knew his tactics. I chose to ignore my intuition when I saw that sly smile. Why did I care what he thought of me? Why do we need to be liked so much by everyone? How did his wanting to make me feel incompetent serve him in his own search for happiness? How could I be a contribution to myself by not taking it personally?

This incident was exactly what I needed to become aware of how I sometimes react to situations, circumstances, and people, instead of consciously respond. I decided I would no longer cut myself into bits or ignore my intuition in order to make someone else feel good. I knew I had always been an excellent, dedicated employee, but in all honesty, I was finished with this work relationship I had created. From this experience I was able to step more fully into who I really am and made the decision that day to recreate my life in a whole new way. I would make my passions and desires the most important aspects of my life. Sometimes we need to be pushed to the brink before we step into our true potential.

There are endless ways in which we give our power away, but the end result is always the same. We feel frustrated, resentful, and powerless. We end up blaming someone or something other than ourselves for our predicament. We give them control over what happens to us.

I'm willing to bet you've given a good bit of your power away today to something you believe is outside of your control.

We love to point blame at everyone and everything else for our pitfalls. I knew something was up when my boss asked if I had copied all the files. I knew I should have asked questions to clarify what he wanted. However, I didn't. I was ready for the fight because mentally I had already moved on and I no longer cared about my role in this company.

People like to play the game of letting outside sources be the cause of their unhappiness. Most people rarely choose to take responsibility for situations, instead believing life is out of their control. They blame their spouse, coworkers, bosses, parents, and even their best friends. They even point blame at their job or a depressing article they read in a magazine—anything they can find to blame. They get so twisted up in their stories of blame that they can't stop thinking about them—allowing them to peck away in their thoughts. They funnel their power into these stories of blame, and the negative energy of it grows while their positive, joyful energy dissipates. Their electricity drains. This continued effort to feed blame can lead to anxiety, depression, self-pity, and shame and rob us of being who we really are! Does this sound familiar?

On a more positive note, when you give your power to something or someone else, they can't use it against you. In fact, no one can use it unless you allow them to. It's a head game! You only think they have control over you. You only think you can't make a move without their permission. In most cases they don't even know you have given your power to them—or how dangerous you could be if you took it back. They have no idea of the mind chatter going on in your thoughts and how much you are feeding this nasty blame monster you've created. How they are acting has nothing to do with you. They have their own things going on—and that's what their actions are all about. They are reacting to the environment they have created, which also includes you.

Everyone in my department knew our boss was overworked and stressed, but he would not let any of us shine or be an example for him. Slowly he pushed everyone away. He took control of everything and became an unpleasant person to work for. Not one of his employees would offer a hand if he asked for it in a time of need. In fact, a mutiny was forming around him, and the only way he could stay afloat was to make everyone else appear to fail. Employee after employee under his supervision quit. I still wonder how long he can keep up this charade without it affecting him personally. My heart reaches out to him. He is an amazing man with vision, but he lacks any understanding of how to motivate a team and use their strengths to his advantage.

We give away our power in so many ways, and unfortunately, it's a common occurrence. Why do we give our power of possibility away, buying into the idea that events must play out in a specific order, before we feel we can go after what we really desire? Let's say for example that you want to start your own business, where you will love being every day because it is driven by your passions. You can visualize it—and in your mind you know how fantastic it is. Thinking of it makes you excited about the new challenges it creates. It is a place where you are motivated. Once you have mapped it out in your mind and are experiencing the feeling of it already being real, you are ready for the next step.

What if you decide to play it safe instead of stepping into it? What if you stay at a job you dislike in order to save up enough money to get things started? What if you pour all of your energy into what you see as your current reality, such as paying off credit cards or paying your monthly bills? What if you look too far into the future, seeing how big your business could become, imagining how much money it could make, and begin to feel overwhelmed?

Playing it safe is how you use your current reality as a roadblock to stop you from getting where you want to go. You give your power to the limiting definition you have bought into as your current reality and don't allow yourself the freedom to jump into this new and exciting adventure. Don't doubt yourself and channel your power into this doubt.

Some people give away their power because they don't like to be the cause of any trouble. These quiet people scare the dickens out of me. I always feel like a ticking time bomb is festering below the surface, waiting to go off. Many women have been taught to be good girls. Good girls are quiet and keep their comments to themselves. These poor things have to live with constantly giving away their power to those who intimidate them. They never speak their truth because they are scared of confrontation. The people who intimidate them will always hold the power because they gladly hand it over to them. Are you one of these people?

Do you spend time with people who are draining? I am always surprised to hear how many women hang on to draining friendships because they "have history together." It's crazy, but I've done it too. There are many reasons why we think we need to hang on to these people, but none of them ever makes any sense when we take a deeper look. I'm not sure why we can't accept that people can grow apart. It can happen in marriages or in friendships. What makes us hold on to people who suck the life out of us because we have common history? When I ask women in this situation why they keep the relationships going, they don't have an answer. They really don't know why. They will make comments like:

- "Whenever I am around her, all she does is talk about all the crap going on in her life." *Translation: Barfs on her friends all the time.*
- "She never calls or returns my calls, and when I do get a hold of her, she gives me a lame excuse about why she didn't call back." *Translation: She's not that into you.*

- "When we do get a chance to talk, it's all about her. She never asks about me, and if I do get the opportunity to get a word in, she suddenly has to get off the phone." *Translation: She's already let you go.*
- "I really hate when we get together, and nothing in her life has changed. She is still depressed, still doesn't know why she's depressed, and is popping drugs like crazy to put a bandage on some nasty boo boo. It drives me crazy!" *Translation: She's already given up on herself and your friendship.*

Why would you continue to hold on to someone who clearly doesn't want anything to do with you? Take your power back and let them go. Not all relationships are meant to last forever. When a marriage breaks up, many friendships do too. It may be a cue that you need to make space for someone new to come into your life.

After all, how can you reinvent yourself without inviting new friends into your life? Just set the old ones free. If those friendships were meant to be, they will transform into something new. I'm not saying to suddenly cut people out of your life by ignoring them or being mean to them. Just let them go in your mind. Let go of every way you are judging and criticizing them. In your mind, set them free. Don't be surprised if they have a total change of heart or if their pessimistic nature gradually changes and they draw you back into their lives in a month or a year. If this happens, follow your gut and listen to your heart.

I know that you desire to be happy and have a fun life. I know you are magnificent and want to feel empowered and energized. I know that through this experience you are feeling caught up in drama and trauma. Step one is to *get real*. This is something most of us are afraid to go head-to-head with, and these power suckers are your excuses to stay in a victim state of mind.

When you give away your power, it is because you feel as if the world causes everything happening around you, instead of you being the cause of those effects. In fact, you are both the cause and the effect, but you only experience being one or the other. The first step to taking back your power is identifying just how you give your power away.

The Thirty Most Common Ways You Give Your Power Away:

1. **Always Say Yes:** You just can't say no. No matter how busy or overscheduled you are, you feel the need to accommodate everyone's requests. Later you create excuses to cancel and get out of your plans. *Translation: I don't like hurting anyone's feelings. It's not nice. I want people to like me.* Saying no always causes trouble. Saying yes all the time puts you at the bottom of your list of priorities. Nothing at the bottom of any list ever gets accomplished. It always gets pushed off to the next day, and the next day, and the next day.

2. **Turning Off Your Emotions:** You plaster on your biggest smile in an effort to fool everyone into believing that you are always happy. *Translation: My problems are small and silly compared to what others are experiencing.* By not paying attention to your emotions, you put yourself at the effect of the world around you. Being vulnerable and sharing how you feel with others creates a human connection. Cutting off your emotions is cutting you off from who you really are.

3. **Settling:** Do you stay in jobs and relationships you hate because you are afraid you can't make it on your own? The fear of the unknown seems far greater than the torture of what you are living now. *Translation: I've never been on my own or made my own decisions. What if I fail?* You ignore your

passions, dreams, and true desires for fear that something worse will happen. You're stuck in the state of mind that "This is the way it is, and everyone else is dealing with it, so I shouldn't expect to be different."

4. **Rarely Doing Things You Enjoy:** You are a people pleaser at heart, and it doesn't feel natural putting your own desires before someone else's. Doing so makes you feel guilty and selfish. *Translation: I don't like conflict.* You give away your right to choose, keep yourself small, and don't cause waves. These are all power suckers that leave you feeling unworthy.

5. **Giving Credit to Everyone Else:** Even when you instigate a project on your own, you can't help but mention anyone who may have contributed. You always feel the need to be humble. You take "working as a team" to a whole new level. *Translation: It wasn't really that great. Everyone else has done it too. I didn't do anything special. I'm not worthy of being noticed.* Not feeling valued will keep you in the background forever. If you don't take credit for what you do, others will. How is this of benefit to you—or them? Being a constant giver will suck the power out of you fast!

6. **Comparing Yourself to Others:** You assume that everyone else is so put together compared to you. You see yourself as a mess, broken, and possibly unfixable. *Translation: I'm not good enough. No matter what I do, I won't be good enough.* Who told you this? Who made you feel this way? At what age did you began to feel this way? Why are you giving this wounded child so much power? How do you know that the people you are comparing yourself to aren't comparing themselves to you?

7. **Negative Self-Language:** This includes such phrases as "I have to," "I never do anything right," "I'm slow," "Nothing

good ever happens to me," "I'm going to do it wrong," "I never win," "I'm hopeless," "I'm not good at doing anything," and "I'm not attractive." *Translation: I don't feel worthy. I don't like who I am.* If you don't blow your own horn, who will? Negative self-language doesn't just suck your power—it's draining on others as well. People see you coming a mile away and detour so they don't have to talk to you. You are, in fact, cutting yourself off big time!

8. **Allowing Others to Dictate What You Do:** Your spouse, parents, children, friends, and employers and even strangers easily manipulate you by instructing you on the right or wrong way to act, and you follow their directions without thought. *Translation: I've never really been allowed to think for myself. Someone has always guided me because I need it.* This is a pattern you adopted at a young age. Somewhere in your life you have an example of someone with a very controlling personality. At that age you handed over your power and continue to do so today. Can you imagine what your life would be like if you made your own decisions?

9. **Not Taking Compliments:** You just can't accept a kind or loving word from anyone without putting yourself down or feeling embarrassed. *Translation: I'm not used to receiving attention. I don't like to be in the spotlight.* Like so many of these power suckers, this is all about self-worth and being seen. Do you realize that by not accepting a compliment, you are not allowing others to be in appreciation of you?

10. **Not Setting Boundaries:** You are afraid of the consequences of setting boundaries. *Translation: People should just be nice and know when they are making hurtful comments to others.* The purpose of setting boundaries is to take care of yourself. You must be able to express when you feel other people

are not acting in ways that are acceptable to you. This is speaking your truth. How you allow others to treat you is your responsibility. Your emotions are a form of internal communication that helps you understand yourself. We are all different, so we need to know from others when we are causing unneeded turmoil.

11. **Believing Your Upbringing Dictates Your Future:** This refers to keeping yourself in a social category because you are afraid to be thought of as different. *Translation: I'm not better than anyone in my family.* This stems from the discussions you heard in your childhood. Did you hear that rich people are snobs? Were you taught that if you don't attend university, you are nobody? Maybe you bought into the idea that without hard work there are no rewards? These are all limitations we buy into in our childhood, without question. What if where you came from was a springboard to greater things?

12. **The Need to Be Liked:** Are you afraid people won't like the real you? *Translation: I have a need to feel loved.* This power sucker is about you cutting yourself off in order to fit into other people's definitions of what they believe life is supposed to look like. If you are obsessed about being liked and can't stand it when someone doesn't like you, you're struggling with self-acceptance.

13. **Taking Everything Personally:** Do you assume there must be some underlying meaning behind what people say and do and that it is projected at you? Do you mistake people's antics for subtle insults? *Translation: I don't like rejection. I don't feel worthy.* Consider the insecurities of who you think is your attacker. What seems to be an attack on you is usually not what it appears to be. Taking everything personally will leave you feeling lifeless.

14. **Hiding behind a Smile:** You pretend to be perfect and happy on the outside, but inside you feel as though your spirit is slowly dying. *Translation: It would be refreshing if someone could actually see me.* Do you really believe that if you plaster on a smile all the time, people can't see the pain in your face and eyes? You are in waiting mode. Waiting to be asked if you are okay. Waiting for someone to want to hear your story. Waiting to be acknowledged. Waiting to be included. Sooner or later you are going to break, and I promise—it won't be pretty!

15. **Expectations:** You feel others should reciprocate in a specific way, or you expect certain actions and behaviors from others. *TranslatioN: I need to be in control.* Expectation will drive you batty! Let me tell you why. When you do something with the expectation of being reciprocated in a specific way and it doesn't show up how you expect it to, you become agitated and angry, and of course, you give away your power.

16. **Lack of Trust:** You often recall past negative examples to judge others. *Translation: I am the victim.* Lack of trust causes arguments and anxiety and decreases self-esteem.

17. **Projecting the Worst Outcome:** You always worry and prepare for the worst. You do this so you won't be disappointed. This locks you into only one or two possible outcomes, blocking other possibilities. *Translation: I don't want to get hurt, so I prepare for the worst.* Why would you choose to cut off the possibility of fantastic outcomes?

18. **The Need for Approval, Appreciation, and Acknowledgment:** *Translation: I fear rejection.* Does your feeling of self-worth depend on what other people think of you? This is a sign of insecurity. Approval, appreciation, and acknowledgment are

wants and desires. They are not emotional needs. Your real power comes from accepting who you are and deciding for yourself what you really want.

19. **Waiting to Have All Your Ducks in a Row:** Everything must be lined up perfectly before you can take action. *Translation: I want to do it right the first time because I may not get another chance.* If you desire a new love relationship and feel the need to lose weight or get in shape instead of concentrating your power into your true desire, you are waiting to have all your ducks in a row. Focusing on something else that you think has to be in place first holds you back from getting what you want.

20. **Playing It Safe:** No risks taken here! *Translation: I do not feel secure.* Most people associate risk with failure. Always playing it safe doesn't allow anything big and exciting to happen in your life. Imagine the excitement of doing something bold that you've always wanted to do and how great that feels. Picture how happy it makes you. Then play it safe. How do you feel now?

21. **Thinking Someone Else Will Make You Happy:** This is something many women were taught at a young age. *Translation: I'm not in charge of my own happiness.* Giving someone else the responsibility for making you happy takes your power away. You feel you are not in charge of your own happiness. Can you see how draining that is?

22. **Caring Too Much about What Others Think:** If you care too much about what others think, allowing them to dictate what is right and wrong, you override what you intuitively know is right for you. You get off course. *Translation: I need approval.* What if what other people think is none of your business?

23. **Buying into Being Ordinary:** Settling for ordinary means not being all of who you are. *Translation: I don't want to stand out.* Do you believe that keeping yourself small is humble? Is the thought of being extraordinary overwhelming? Being extraordinary is not beyond your means. Do you underestimate what you are capable of? The only thing that is limiting you from being extraordinary is you.

24. **Putting All Your Eggs into One Basket:** Do you put all of your efforts and hopes into only one conclusion? *Translation: I get stuck on one thing and can't see beyond it.* Are you willing to lose everything if you drop that basket? If you drop that basket, beating yourself up is sure to follow.

25. **Choosing to Believe It's Too Late:** This is a power sucker many people fall prey to. Do you believe that if you haven't accomplished something by a certain age, your dream is shattered? *Translation: There is only so much time.* This is a lack mind-set. Why not release yourself from lack and plug into what's happening now? That is where all your power is.

26. **Focusing on What You Believe Are Your Weaknesses:** This is a common power sucker. *Translation: I can always improve.* There is nothing about you to improve—but tons to *expose.* Focusing on your weaknesses keeps you small. There are many things to learn, and it's ultimately up to you to choose how you want to explore them. How you do that comes from your inner knowing. Focus on your strengths, take back your power, and forget about all that weakness crap.

27. **Being Indecisive:** "Should I do this or that? What are the pros and cons? How do I decide?" *Translation: I'm afraid of failure and judgment.* This way of thinking boxes you in. In the first five seconds of having the opportunity to make a decision,

you know the true answer. After that initial five seconds, ego steps in and screws everything up, recalling negative examples that keep you from reaching a decision. Can't you just feel how draining it is to jump back and forth and never make a decision? Whew! I'm tired just thinking about it.

28. **Seeing Yourself as the Savior:** You might think it's not only good but admirable to give of yourself for the sake of another. You may do this because of past pain or conflict. *Translation: I'm not fixable.* Those who feel the need to save others often feel they themselves are broken. Do you believe that if you can do it right for someone else, it will exonerate you from your own pain? It is essential that you allow others to walk their own path.

29. **Judgment:** When you obsess over what you perceive as someone else's bad behavior, or just plain get off from making other people miserable, it's like bowing down and calling them master! *Translation: I'm not happy.*

30. **Needing Someone Else to Feel Whole and Complete:** When you are swept off your feet, you feel alive and turned on. There is nothing wrong with passion as long as you don't give your heart away completely. You need to be a *me* before you can be a *we*. There are always three relationships when two people choose to be a couple: your relationship with you, the other person's relationship with themselves, and the relationship born between the both of you. *Translation: I'm lonely.*

Do any of these sound familiar? It's powerful to realize that only you can give away your power. It may feel like a slap in the face when you recognize you have been allowing others to control your actions and decisions, but coming to that realization is a huge aha moment. These actions are really reactions or patterns you have learned to play over and over again. In knowing this, you now have the opportunity to take your power back. As you discover these patterns, you will become a new you. Life will be different. You will be different. In recognizing these old patterns, you begin to release them. Soon you will be a whole new woman. Aren't you excited?

Every time I discover another way I am handing my power over to someone or something else, I feel lighter and more expansive. At first, it pisses me off to think I allowed myself to get caught up in something for so long. Eventually I see how I can take back my power and the responsibility for making my own decisions—without the limitation of what anyone else thinks about my choices.

I too used to give my power away because of old patterns. The man I am currently dating told me he was changing his long-distance phone plan to a cheaper one so we could talk longer. His text to me read, "Girlfriend is expensive ... but worth it."

I froze, my chest felt heavy, and a rush of past conversations with my ex flooded my thoughts. Declarations of how *expensive* I was and being blamed for always spending money foolishly rushed at me. I suddenly felt vulnerable. My ex had pinched and saved every penny. He had viewed eating at a restaurant or a night at the movies as a waste of money. For years, our only holiday was a staycation, and home renovations were seen as useless expenses.

A huge lump formed in my throat, and I did my familiar swallowing technique to prevent myself from crying. *Did he really say that? Does he really think of me as an expense?* I was mortified. I had been reduced to an expense in a man's life again. My stomach churned. My heart told me this loving man did not intend to make me feel this way, but I could not control my feelings. I had given away my power because of this belief I had bought into.

I believed I was not worthy of receiving loving attention, and I was unknowingly supporting this belief with my actions. When my new lover and I went out to dinner, I offered to contribute half to the bill as a way of proving I was not taking advantage of him. I felt terrible every time he cooked me wonderful meals, knowing I was not spending nearly as much on the meals I prepared for him because I was enforcing a strict cutback on my groceries in order to save every penny. I was digging a hole of "lack of money" deeper and deeper within my subconscious because I never again wanted to be viewed as someone's burden.

Wow! That sure came out of nowhere! I realized how I had given money the power to make me feel insecure and unworthy of having or receiving nice things. My ex rarely bought me flowers or gave unexpected gifts. Even in my last relationship, I was rather shocked at the gifts I received from my lover. He would give me sample bottles of shampoo and conditioner from fancy hotels he stayed in.

This *lack* monster I had created was not serving me, and it showed up far too often. What transpired within me was not the intention of my lover. He simply wanted us to be able to talk on the phone more frequently, but the patterns his words connected to within me were draining.

I hope you now have a better understanding of how you give away your power. It is my intention to get your creative juices flowing so you can uncover some of the ways you disempower yourself—and how you can begin to take some of that power back. It is a process; don't be hard on yourself if you find you are in the middle of a power-draining scenario and don't know how to stop it. You've learned the pattern, and this is the time to be patient with yourself, engage curiosity, and ask questions. Soon you will feel more confident in these situations as you begin to take more and more of your power back.

Don't scold yourself for giving away your power or blame someone for being cruel enough to take it. Recognize that the process is unfolding. Feeling good about the decisions you make and knowing they are *your* decisions will help you to feel empowered and in control as a single, forty-plus woman.

Chapter Nine
HIDDEN GEMS

You've reached an unexpected point in life. How many times have you wondered, *Is this really it?* I have said those four words at least a hundred times since leaving my ex.

When I feel that way, I say, "What happened to all the fun stuff I had planned? What happened to having money and traveling all over the world? What happened to opening my business and helping others discover themselves and their passions? What happened to freedom? Is this it? Really? Get up, go to work, hate my job, risk losing it, get home, eat, do laundry, write, play video games, walk the dog, sleep, and do it all again? Seriously?"

Sometimes I think the world is swirling around me. I often find it difficult to believe I am a part of anything when I am at home alone. Have you ever felt this way? I live on the top floor of my building; at this moment, there are three people alone on their balconies. Two are men, and one is me—a two-to-one ratio.

It amazes me when I look across the cityscape at the beautiful July greenness and the houses speckled in between. The trees are gently swaying in the fresh summer breeze. I'm aware that people are outside enjoying their backyards with barbeques and swimming pools. Some are walking their dogs, taking their children to baseball games, or getting ready to go to the movies with friends—or a new lover. I am alone.

I'm sure many women in similar situations feel this way periodically. Sometimes being alone is depressing. At other times, when I feel this way, I set off to the bookstore and wander around with a latte to pick up my spirits. Loneliness can creep up without you noticing. Most days, I focus my energy on viewing the world through rose-colored glasses. It all depends on the types of interactions I have with people—and my personal sense of awareness when the day begins. When I hone in on the drama in other people's lives (politics, religion, fear, messages from the media, paying attention to others complaining about what the media is saying, constant grumbling about the weather, or nagging about the latest virus or flu infecting everyone), I'm not a happy camper. It's easy to get sucked into that vibe when everyone is constantly protesting and criticizing.

The other day, a woman joined me in the elevator on the way up to my apartment. We greeted each other, and she remarked how she felt it was much too hot outside. She shared how they were forecasting an awfully hot summer. I can't tell you how much this weather talk gets under my skin. When people can't come up with something to complain about, they start griping about the weather.

With a huge smile, I replied, "Today was a perfect day, and the heat is much better than snow. We don't have to wear boots and bundle up from head to toe when we go outside. I love the way it is right now."

She let the tiniest smile sneak across her lips as she contemplated my opinion. As we arrived at her floor, she stepped off the elevator, turned to me, and said, "I guess we better enjoy it while we have it because it won't last long!"

I was dumbfounded. As the elevator door slid shut behind her, I smiled. I realized that this summer was going to be the most incredible and exciting one ever for me. I imagined it full of unexpected and wonderful experiences. I found it unfortunate that this beautiful, bountiful season may pass by for her without any notice—except for the weather forecast.

Although drama sometimes swirls around in my head like it has a life of its own, I often catch it in the act and put an end to it before it leads me down the nasty path of limitation. I go through cycles where I buy into the things I hear and see—and I don't even realize I'm getting all caught up in it. When I become aware of the visions and thoughts running rampant in my mind, I stop it. It really doesn't take much energy to stop unpleasant thoughts. You just become aware that they are zipping around as if you have hooked up zip lines throughout your brain—there—and then gone! There—and then gone! Then you focus on something joyful.

What if everything that has occurred in your life could be defined as having been absolutely perfect?

When you pay attention, negative thoughts can be brought entirely to a halt. All it takes is a little effort to choose to focus on thoughts that bring a smile to your face. It's all in how you choose to interpret things. You may be accustomed to defining your life as busy, tiresome, routine, out of control, or boring. Everything that has occurred in your life could be defined as having been absolutely perfect. I'm not kidding! I know this is not what you've been taught to believe. How could it be perfect? If it was, you would have all kinds of cool stuff— and that's not the case, is it? If it was, you would be married and living happily ever after, still madly in love with your ex. But you aren't. If it was perfect, all this terrible stuff would not have happened.

Can you imagine your life with no challenges, no differences of opinion, no foul color schemes, and no crazy, screaming drivers? It would be blissful, loving, fun, exciting, and wonderful. All of that can be yours if you let go of your old points of view and relax into the joy and comfort of where you are in your life right now. Instead, when your life is flowing along nicely, your mind chatter says, "When is the ball going to drop?"

What if it was true? What if everything you have experienced up until this very second has been absolutely perfect?

- What if you could see all of your life experiences in a timeline sprawled out in front of you? What if it revealed that every decision you have ever made was perfect instead of focusing on what you have chosen to call failures, mistakes, or bad decisions?
- What if events didn't just happen to you? What if you had control of everything in your life? What if these events were mini creations on their way to exposing something even more wonderful?
- What if you have a mean, annoying boss because you believe all bosses are mean and nasty—and you can't imagine one acting any differently?
- What if you have friends who take advantage of you because you believe people have, and always will, walk all over you?

- What if you always struggle with a lack of money because you are a chronic worrier and live in fear of not being able to look after yourself—just as your parents struggled?

Aren't these all choices? Examine your history with curiosity and from the point of view that with every life experience you have exposed more of who you truly are instead of buying into the idea that everything is out of your control.

If you've been taught to get used to things because it's just the way things are, this will seem completely nuts. Have you taken some of the ideas from this book to heart and begun to expand your way of thinking? What if, at a very young age, you adopted the idea that "life just happens to me," but there was also the possibility that "nothing is a coincidence"?

While I was still employed in that toxic work environment, one of my friends and I had a conversation. I was sharing another story about my new boss, enlightening her about how much trouble I was having adapting to working with his overbearing, strictly work, no-fun, minimul-praise management style.

My friend said, "Surely the owners of the company will put two and two together when they see everyone is miserable and realize they have just replaced one person with the same personality? Everyone can't hate this man without the owners being aware of it!"

I replied, "What does it matter? If they get rid of him, they will only replace him with some other tyrant who could even be worse!"

My friend quickly saw the error in my thinking and pointed out my limiting belief and negative point of view regarding bosses.

I had to agree. I could not remember working for an employer who was friendly and loving. The work environments I experienced all consisted of owners and managers who yelled, belittled, provided little or no direction, and expected overtime without pay. My friend's experiences had been quite the opposite. Her bosses provided encouragement, guidance, friendship, and trust. I couldn't imagine such a thing!

I learned that these experiences had provided me with little hidden gems—as long as I was willing to expect and receive them. These hidden gems were usually not discovered until a series of events were completed. That is when you can see that your life consists of strings of perfect choices that lead you to the people, places, opportunities, and experiences to expand who you are and expose more of yourself.

Most people draw conclusions based on the worst possible examples of stuff they have lived through, and they use this to define their whole lives. They give credit to the unpleasant experiences instead of observing the hidden gems that are nestled inside.

Humans focus so intently on the negative, overlooking the fact that there are so many more positive events in our lives. It's as if we are attempting to live up to something we think is bigger and better. We compare ourselves continuously to something we think we can never be. We merely can't see what's good, joyful, or loving about our lives. What if we are already perfect the way we are? What if we actually chose the awful experiences? What if, as a photograph emerges slowly and reveals itself in a darkroom, we chose how much of ourselves we allowed to be exposed at one time?

Take a moment to do a quick scan of your life. You've taken chances and leaps of faith. You have made mistakes and lived through them. What if right now you are in the perfect place? What if you could step back and see the experiences of your life from beginning to end, including the events about to be exposed, on a big timeline in front of you? Do you know what you might see?

- You might discover how all of the great paths you chose and desired to experience have assisted you in exposing who you came here to be.
- You might <u>discover</u> how a series of events led you to a perfect outcome—even if it felt like a struggle along the way.
- You might be amazed by how your choices have affected others.
- You might understand how choosing to let something devastating happen brought you to something wonderful.

I've been thinking a lot about this lately and am excited about how much more I can <u>experience</u>. When you look back over the events of your life, it's easy to see how they are nothing more than a connection of choices—even if you believe many of the choices were decided for you by someone else. Of course you would be fooling yourself, but this is what most people have chosen to believe is reality. Choosing to let it happen was a <u>choice</u>. Moment after moment, you make choices. When a series of choices and events are completed, a brilliant <u>gem</u> is revealed.

Let's Go Gem Hunting

Imagine if it was your life's mission to uncover these hidden gems? What if you knew such gems existed in all life experiences and were waiting to be discovered? How would this knowledge change your life? During the times when everything appears to be crumbling around you, when life's dramas were bringing you to your knees, you knew you would pull through and that something <u>spectacular</u> would reveal itself. Your viewpoint on life would be <u>completely</u>

different. Your existence would blow your mind. You wouldn't be so serious about everything. You would have faith and would <u>believe</u> your choices were perfect. You would take responsibility for your actions, and it would be tremendous.

A very good friend asked me the most simple yet complex question. He asked if I was happy. I paused for what seemed the longest time before answering. These first seconds after being asked such a question are the most crucial. There are approximately five seconds ... tick, tick, tick, tick, tick ... where the topic makes contact with a higher level within you—and the true answer is revealed. You clearly know the answer—without any <u>doubts</u>.

After this, your ego jumps in with evidence from past experiences and examples to support a negative conclusion. It switches you from a knowing state of mind to an analyzing state of mind. When you start analyzing, everything begins to get sketchy. Analyzing takes you to a totally different place—<u>intellectually</u> and emotionally. You conjure up all sorts of past experiences and recreate them as new ones in your body. If you didn't enjoy them the first time, they are no more fun the second or third time around.

Once the question was asked, I instantaneously knew the answer. No! In that moment, I recognized that I was not being my authentic self. I chose to keep most of who I am hidden from what I saw as the outside world. I would bend who I was in order to <u>match</u> what others viewed as acceptable and normal. Although I knew I had lived through many joyful experiences, I did not believe I was following a course that would take me to the wonderful adventures I wished for. I did feel as though I was at a <u>place</u> in my life where I was letting go and leaving something behind that no longer served me.

The question was a hidden gem. It was presented at the perfect time. Instead of letting my ego sneak in to take me down Bad

Choices Memory Lane, I chose to look at all of the wonderful aspects of my life.

- Being with my son; talking, laughing, going to the bookstore, and playing video games.
- The realization that I really like who I am. Self-exploration has helped me expose more of the pieces I've kept hidden away, and it has helped me release some self-judgment. I can now see the advantages of hanging out with myself.
- I enjoy conversations with just about anyone—waitresses, bellboys, the person helping me board the train, or the sales clerk assisting me in choosing the perfect dress. I adore all of the people at Starbucks who helped me learn how to order my latte in Starbucks language (Venti, half-sweet, soy Tazo Chai). It took me three months of weekly visits to get it right. Connections with people on this level inspire me. They are so simple and perfect. It surprises me how others have not caught on to this great vibration.
- I love the analyzer in me. She likes to explore new ideas and isn't tied tightly to any one point of view. She is open to what is possible.
- I adore the incredible women in my life. I have surrounded myself with the most loving, inspiring, thoughtful, honest, brilliant, and creative women. I cherish each of them dearly.
- Incredible experiences continuously burst forth before me. Whenever I think I am stuck or lost, someone or some event reaches out to show me another marker on my path or another fork in my road to choose from. It always has such perfect timing.
- I love my creativity. I could spend hours writing, doodling, or painting.
- The choices I made regarding my career have made a huge contribution to my life. I have had the joy of working with a

number of different personalities who have taught me to see the world from different perspectives. Most importantly, the life experiences generated from these careers have created a desire in me to do business differently by creating work environments using people's strengths instead of pointing out their weaknesses.

- People come and go throughout my life—and that's okay. I have moved seventeen times—with more to come. These moves included leaving people behind and having to make new friends. From this, I have developed the ability to read people from a distance and attract people who will contribute to my life—and I to theirs.

In order to redefine yourself, it is essential to give credit to everything you have right now. Find the big gem, or many little gems, from the roads you have traveled. Make it your mission to take back every bit of your power so you can be fully present in your body. Those so-called terrible events are blessings in disguise. You can't look back and connect the dots until you have gone through the string of events.

People say, "If I had not done A, then B would not have happened, which led me to meet him, and then C happened."

Suddenly it's all very clear. There are oodles of gems scattered throughout your life, and most people have never bothered to give them any attention.

The Jealousy Trap

In my early twenties, I got caught up in jealousy. I was struggling in a relationship with a man my parents disapproved of, and my best friend was joyfully planning her wedding. It appeared that she didn't have extra time for me, and I became quite jealous of her happiness.

This led me to do something completely out of character. I began to spread hurtful lies about her behind her back. The lies and gossip swiftly attracted attention. People were suddenly paying attention to what I was saying, and I started to feel better while I stole some of my friend's glory.

I soon became concerned about the lies I was spreading. I wondered how I would react if my friend confronted me. The fact that she was busy planning her wedding made it easy to avoid the subject, but what was I going to feel like the next time we were together? I wondered what had ever possessed me to be so cruel. Suddenly, the answer was clear. By asking myself what would ever possess me to want to ruin my best friend's happiness, I knew the answer. I was ashamed of my actions. I suddenly understood that by doing what I could to destroy her happiness, I somehow felt a little better about my own predicament. I traded some of her joy to get some for myself.

I knew there was a possibility that my friend would not accept my apology. I also knew that coming clean was the best choice for me. If she chose to remove me from her friend list forever, then so be it. What happened was completely the opposite. She wrapped her arms around me—with the love friends have for each other—and told me she had heard I was spreading rumors and was about to confront me. She understood my jealousy and forgave me immediately. In her opinion, it was rare for any person to admit to such doings and willingly receive whatever consequences were dealt to them. In her eyes, I was a true friend.

What was the hidden gem? I expanded <u>considerably</u> by confessing my actions. I also learned I have a vicious side. Jealousy is indeed a quality of my personality. I am thankful I was able to see how mean I was being to another person, I am proud that I chose to come clean—no matter what the cost was to my ego. Recognizing that the outcome may not result in my favor was akin to knowing that you sometimes have to take a bullet, heal, and move on. I also discovered the magic of telling the truth—and that people can forgive and love.

One Thing Led to Another

Years ago, I held hands with a world of negativity, pain, and suffering, and I slipped into a depression that lasted nearly two years. I also began to experience bouts of insomnia, and I often stayed awake until two, three, or five o'clock. One night, an itching <u>sensation</u> crept over my entire body. I began to vigorously rub my arms, and soon my entire body felt as if it was on fire. I jumped out of bed and began to pace in the hallway. I rubbed and scratched at my arms and legs. It was overwhelming, and it was well into the wee hours of the morning before I collapsed onto the couch.

A friend explained that it sounded like an anxiety attack. She told me to seek help, but I ignored her advice. Over the following weeks, my condition worsened. The next stage was a complete lack of enthusiasm. I slowly pushed everyone away. Although I tried to hide my lack of feelings, it was difficult. Every night, I shut myself away in our sun room and stared into the yard. Negative thoughts ran through my mind. *Why am I here? What is the purpose for living in such a cruel place where we slaughter animals and eat them without any regard for how terrified they are while they are dying? Where we pick on even our own, and abuse and belittle them. We destroy our planet without even a <u>thought</u>! Why would I choose to live in such a place? What is my purpose here?*

With so much negativity and hopelessness, I considered ending my life. The idea felt completely natural, and I genuinely felt my husband and son would be better off without me. I have a hard time admitting these thoughts, but they are far from who I am today.

It was also at this time I became intrigued by the hands-on healing arts, and I was introduced to a Reiki Master. She was wonderful and loving, and I immediately adored her. Her energy felt so different than mine did.

She said, "You don't feel like you really belong here, do you? You feel very uncomfortable in your skin, literally, don't you?"

When I agreed, she suggested a book to read that she felt would help me, and we scheduled a time for me to experience a Reiki treatment.

I rushed out to purchase the book, but it was out of stock. I chose another title by the same author and ordered the one she had suggested. What happened was perfect. When I couldn't sleep, I read. While I read, the same questions ran around in my head, and I realized that the words I was reading felt as if *I* had written them. My thoughts—and my conversations with my husband that had bored him to tears—were written in that book. How could it be? Everything I was reading felt like complete truth. As I read, I continued to ask myself why I would come to such a place. Joy was the word that finally came to mind.

What was the hidden gem? The sequence of events led me through grief—to becoming interested in the New Age healing techniques—to someone who led me to a book—to the idea of a joyful life—to a journey of self-empowerment. This string of events taught me to trust in myself. I shifted emotionally from despair to hope. I understood it was not life that was responsible for my feelings—I was! Everything was about me! I chose to feel unworthy and lost. I chose to look at life through tainted glasses. I was responsible. I understood that if I changed my attitude toward how I perceived life, my experiences would be more pleasing. From that point on, I chose to change my way of thinking in order to begin the journey toward feeling better.

Knowing these gems are scattered throughout my life has helped me stay open to other possibilities as my life progresses. Hundreds of other gems have helped me grow into the independent, loyal, loving, intuitive life coach I am today. I often wonder who I would <u>be</u> if I had not discovered the value of expecting wonderful outcomes from my life experiences.

Ending any marriage takes a lot of courage. Many women are ashamed and carry so much guilt during separation and divorce. They have a difficult time moving forward. I have come to realize, as I hope you will also, that all healthy relationships begin with you. The primary relationship must be with you—before you can ever start searching for a mate or any relationship. When you can look back at everything you have accomplished from the point where you stepped out on your own, no matter how it happened to come about, you will discover the hidden gems from the whole experience.

The hidden gems are waiting for you to discover them.

It's too bad your mama didn't tell you they were there in the first place. If she had, you would be embracing all of the wonderful, joyful experiences unfolding in front of you. Think back to a time when you were extremely proud of something. There is a gem there, and what you will most likely find attached to it is risk.

Risk plays a huge role in our lives, but it isn't always big and dramatic. In one circumstance, the risk was following my gut and telling the truth. In the second scenario, the risk I embraced was trust. Trusting someone I had just met was not my nature back then, but I took a chance.

We often associate risk with extreme, life-altering situations where we must make painful choices. In truth, most risks aren't a big deal or a huge threat. Taking a risk means there is potential for an undesirable outcome, and that belief can stop us in our tracks. You may have taken risks without knowing the outcome:

- Choosing a career to study in college or university. You may have hated your choice and had to return to the drawing board, but it all works out in the end.
- Receiving three job offers—and having to choose one. There is always risk involved in taking a job. Who knows if you will like it? But you make a choice and take the risk.
- Getting married is a big risk, but it's nothing you can't live through.
- Getting pregnant. Some wouldn't call it a risk, but raising children is always risky. Nobody knows what the outcome will be, but we go for it anyways. It could have something to do with all the hidden gems we are expecting along the way.
- Making a career change is a big risk. Around this age, many of us choose to jump ship and refocus our lives strictly for joy.
- Telling your best friend a truth they may not want to hear or that might hurt their feelings. This is a very common risk.
- Investing money. Risk is written all over it, but some people just love it.
- Gambling is like throwing money in the trash with the huge hope of winning enough to start a new life. It is risky, but it can be quite fun.

You are already taking risks. You cannot take a risk without learning, growing, and evolving. It just cannot be! Can you remember a time when you took a risk—and the payoff was amazing and changed your life? I dare you to record some of them in your journal. Finding them is a great way to feel good about you. It is an incredible feeling to look at a situation from a different perspective and discover something wonderful about it.

Why not get mining now?

Chapter Ten
THE FORKS IN YOUR ROADS AHEAD

Being single is an adjustment. I am still getting used to this new lifestyle; in my case, transitioning from being married to becoming single wasn't an enormous shift. I was already spending most of my free time on my own. I actually like my own space and enjoy meditating in absolute quiet. I adore spending cold winter mornings sweeping paint-filled brushes across a new canvas or creating a new painting while looking out across the city from my window. Using the tools I share in this book, I have learned the importance of paying attention to how I feel at all times—and acknowledging any negative mind chatter I am holding on to.

This much silence can feel frightening. You may never have experienced living alone, and this single situation feels uncomfortable. Do you prefer constant noise in the background while driving, cleaning the house, or sitting on your patio? For those whose lives were centered on children's activities, it can be apparent how much of your free time they occupied. If your children's schedules are no longer playing center stage, having so much time to yourself could seem somewhat uncomfortable.

You are still you, but you are more seasoned by life. Notice I didn't say *older*. You are still young! Age is merely a number. A great advantage of being single at this beautiful age, after everything you have lived through in your twenties and thirties, is that you don't have as much to prove to anyone! You no longer have to justify your actions to your parents, friends, or lovers. How cool is that? How about not having the stress of someone else's baggage? Your ex might be causing difficulties, but at least you are not in each other's space any longer, pretending or faking your feelings.

How about your in-laws? If you had terrible in-laws, you don't have to deal with them on the same scale any longer. Woot! Woot! This has never been an issue for me. My in-laws are amazing people, but I know a ton of women who say they would love to divorce their in-laws. Now you just have to worry about your own crazy family!

You've led yourself to this experience. You've traveled a road and made choices that have taken you to this moment. Change your perspective and look at your life in a new way. Take charge of your life and enjoy how perfect your circumstance is. It's puberty again— but with brains and more money. If you are experiencing the next change in a woman's life, then more than ever you have entered a portal back to puberty. It is like when you were in your teens, and your life could unfold in countless ways. This is the time to reengage your passions, your soul, and the real you before anything else can change in your life.

Now is the time to do some serious soul listening.

How do you listen to your soul? How do you engage your spirit? It's really very simple. You ask! The best way I have found to start listening to your soul is by keeping a journal.

Journaling can connect you with your passions and spirit. Some people hate keeping a journal or don't enjoy writing; you may already be turning up your nose to the idea. You are at a place in life where many choices are available to you. There are more open doors in front of you, right now, than you can imagine. You might not be able to see the opportunities available because you may feel that more opportunities have been stolen from you than have been given to you. This is not true. That's your ego leading you down a limited, familiar path.

Raise your arms in front of you with your palms facing down. Spread your fingers wide and touch the tips of your thumbs together. Look at your fingers. Each finger represents an opportunity and a different choice for every single life experience you encounter. Each is beneficial—no matter what challenges await. Some offer a rockier road to travel compared to others, but all have hidden gems for you to discover. You get to choose a path with bumps or one that feels like smooth sailing. As you hold your hands in this manner, it's easy to see how you are the connecting factor. All your choices lead back to you. You've led yourself to this situation, and the forks in your road are all new. New adventures and possibilities are waiting for you. Some you can imagine, but others would never cross your mind.

Whenever you wonder what will happen next, hold up your hands in this way and connect with the idea that there are an infinite number of paths you can choose to get to any destination or desire. You are not limited to ten choices just because you have ten fingers. The possibilities are endless and infinite, but this little trick will help you open your awareness to the idea that there are more than a couple of ways that any circumstance can play out.

Look for the door that is presenting itself; it is waiting for you to open it and step through into a new quest. Random thoughts will pop into your thoughts. *What if I did this? I could do that!* As they pop in, your ego will instinctively reach for familiar experiences to compare them with. Ego calls upon the familiar by pulling from memories of past events and happenings. It might captivate you with the idea of finding a new partner who will provide you with security—rather than being with someone just for the fun of it— because that's what you feel you lacked in your prior relationship. It may engulf you with thoughts that make you believe you are not worthy or try to convince you that every road in front of you is a punishment. It pulls data from your core beliefs and definitions, but you're on a new quest. You are unraveling your core beliefs and reinventing who you are because they are your old stories. In order to rebuild, you have to tear something apart.

Writing in a journal can help unlock some of those doors. Your subconscious desire for joy puts these magical doors in front of you, but you, my gorgeous friend, have to open them and walk through them. The key to your subconscious is unlocking blocks and allowing you to be aware of your thoughts and feelings right now. This is where you want to be! Journaling provides a viewable history. When you keep a record of your experiences, you become aware of how the dots connect, which allows you to make positive choices that steer you toward a desired result. This method reveals your progress and sticking points. It records where you have traveled and where you are most likely going. It keeps you in check with your emotions, and it provides you with proof that you are changing and moving forward.

Start by purchasing a nice journal. Choose one you love that resonates with you when you hold it. You'll know it when you see it. If you prefer, use your computer to journal. You could go to www. idonethis.com and use the free version of the site as your daily journal; it is perfect for those who need daily e-mail reminders. You could also start a new text document. Choose whatever option is the most comfortable for you.

This is not a barf journal. Some people use journals to keep a daily log of events that usually consist of negative comments. You are not to write about adverse events of the day or the details of any horror stories you lived before this point. This exercise is about looking ahead, moving forward, detailing how you feel, and reaching for even better feelings.

The key to journaling is to give time back to you. It's important to document your emotions at the time you are journaling (keeping the barf to a minimum) and keeping notes regarding how you want to feel. Use this opportunity to rediscover some of the wonderful things about you and your life. Each time you journal, ask yourself, "How am I feeling right now, and what would it take to feel even better?" This question shifts you out of lack and into what is possible. Don't enter the details of why you feel the way you do. Instead, mention how much better you could feel. Remember—forward, not backward.

Here are some ways to journal for those ready to jump right in:

- **Just write.** Put pen to paper and write. Don't take your pen off the paper or worry about punctuation, spelling, or grammar. Just write. Ask yourself a question and let your emotions pour out of you onto the paper. If you have nothing to say, write "I have nothing to say." Ask yourself why—and see what comes to you. The idea is to simply write whatever comes to mind.
- **Ask questions.** Write as if you and a good friend are chatting. "So Catherine, what's up today? How are you feeling? What's on your mind? What's the best thing that happened to you today? What do you feel are your obstacles? Where

would you like to travel next? What are you doing lately that engages your creative spirit?"

- **Get creative.** Another way to have fun with journaling is to use crayons or colored pencils. Express your feelings with color. Doodle or scribble. What colors are you attracted to today? If you can only draw stick people, then stick (no pun intended) to that. Fill the paper with color. Use color to make you feel good!

- **Scrapbook.** This is another way to engage your spirit in your journal. Get some recent photos, ticket stubs, receipts, or leaves. Choose anything uplifting. You don't have to write words; simply engage your spirit as you add these treasures to your journal pages.

- **With intent.** Journal with intent. Start off your week searching for anything that brings you joy and keep a record of it. If it doesn't make you feel good, walk away and search for something that does. Keep a record of your findings. Joy is everywhere if you open your senses to receiving it. Look at architecture; write about the smell of the air or how you said thank you to someone.

- **Acting as if.** This is a fun way to get in the mind-set of your future. Pretend you are already living the life of your dreams. Don't try reaching too far out or it will feel like an unattainable goal. Go on a quest and write from the viewpoint of already being there. This is a lot of fun and puts you in a great space emotionally. I do it often. *Today in my penthouse; Today at my book signing; Today opening my new business; Today in Italy; Today as a lottery winner; Today at my speaking engagement; Today with my lover.*

- **To find possibilities.** Sometimes we are confused about situations. This is usually the time when we reach out to others for answers. That's not going to help since the answers others give are not for you—they are for *them.* Their advice is based on their past experiences, beliefs, and training. Start with yourself to see what you come up with.

I tell my clients that they can find all their answers within themselves. When you incorporate this as a truth, new possibilities reveal themselves. Have you ever been puzzled about something in your life, but once it was resolved, you felt as if you knew the answer all along?

When you are in the heart of what appears to be a difficult situation, work through it in your journal first. If you have recently gone through something difficult, spend some time reflecting (not barfing). Don't try to figure out what the lesson from the experience is. That thought often shifts people into self-blame. Instead, play with the magic of wonder and think of the bigger picture. Write about it in your journal. *I wonder what the importance of this occurrence is in the bigger scheme of things. I wonder how this situation can be a contribution to me now and in my future. I wonder what amazing hidden gems I can find if I look for them. I wonder what other possibilities there are that I can even imagine.*

For those of you who are not lovers of journaling, keep in mind that this is a fun exercise. Some people think keeping a journal is a constant endeavor. Although that process can be fun for those who actually enjoy it, your objective is to reconnect with your true self and rediscover a few more pieces in the mystery of who you are. Journaling is one of the most beneficial ways to do this.

Journaling provides an outlet for self-expression and can be a great stress reliever. It's a way of getting your thoughts outside of you—much like talking about them to someone. We often bottle issues up and keep our true feelings to ourselves, which can be dangerous. Writing them down helps the body release some of what it is holding on to. It makes you feel as though you are looking for a solution instead of barfing the same old story. It also helps you focus on what is most important now, and it gives you proof of how you are progressing.

What I like about journaling is that I am making time for me. It actually forces me to make time for myself! Your journal is a message from your heart, which is not something many people engage in these days.

Fourteen-Day Joy Journal Challenge

For those of you who are new to journaling, I thought it might be helpful to get started with a fun fourteen-day joy journal challenge. New and different is what we are going for.

Day One—The First Time

Label today's jounal entry: **I Remember the First Time I**. In today's exercise, recall a memorable moment when you enjoyed something for the first time. It could be trying a new food, the day you got your first pet, the first time you traveled on a plane, or the first time you met someone. Anything. Take time to remember all the good feelings around this time—and write about it in your journal. Pay attention to how you feel while you are writing and recalling this wonderful, first-time event in your life. It's a fantastic feeling! Don't push through it to get it done. Write down all the joyful details. Include information leading up to the event, the actual event, and how you felt after the event, but only record the positive aspects.

Day Two—Spirit Booster

Label today's jounal entry: **Things That Arouse My Spirit**. This journal exercise is all about connecting with the energy of everything that awakens your spirit—and I don't mean coffee! Some things that arouse my spirit are the smell of fresh air; the sound trees make when the wind rustles their leaves in summer (which sounds like ocean waves meeting the beach to me); lying on the grass and watching the clouds; shopping in a craft shop for new exciting paint colors to splash on a blank canvas; cuddling on the couch with Chester Pug; searching for new information on the Internet; snorkeling in the ocean; deep conversations; laughing with friends; and taking a long, hot shower. Write down everything that you love—even if it's silly. This exercise will make you feel good while doing it—and who doesn't love feeling good? Doing this also puts you into a vibe of appreciation and abundance. Expect some wonderful things to manifest today!

Day Three—ABCD

Label today's jounal entry: **Empowerment**. Your quest today is to create sentences about you that start with each letter of the word empowerment. Each sentence must contain positive, empowering words about you. You get to talk about all your good qualities. Nothing negative can be written. Positive sentence #1 starts with E. Positive sentence #2 starts with M. Positive sentence #3 starts with P, and so on. Have fun!

Here is my fun rant:

Excellence surrounds me in the people I work and play with.

Manifestation is easy for me now that I know I am the creator of all my life experiences.

Pleasure is my quest every day!

Opportunities pop up just when I want them to.

Wow. I love who I am!

Everything I've ever dreamed of is coming true.

Remembering who I am is so much better than pretending to be someone else.

Making a difference in other people's lives is a rich gift to me.

Extra hidden gems keep popping up in my life.

Nothing is going to stop me from being all of who I am ever again.

Today, I love who I am, and I will share me with as many people as possible.

Day Four—Fear Be Gone

Label today's jounal entry: **Fearless Me**. Who would you be if you had no fear? I've let you have so much fun over the last three days, but this exercise is a bit more challenging. It will help you discover any blocks that are holding you back. The best part of journaling is that you begin to learn more and more about yourself. Take your time. Don't pressure yourself. Identify one of your fears and visualize how your life would be different if you didn't have it. Write from the position of being fearless. Come up with at least three fears you could do without. Choose ones that would change your life.

Day Five—Decluttering

Label today's jounal entry: **Five Things I Could Do Without**. It's time to throw out the trash—literally! How can you make room in your life for new and exciting experiences if you are surrounded by stuff? Today's assignment is to identify ten objects you could get rid of and list them in your journal. Don't go to your closet, pull out ten old sweaters, and think you are done with this exercise. Walk around your home and choose five items that you really don't need. Did they have a purpose at one time but could use a new home?

The next step is to determine why you've held on to them. What purpose did they have? What attachments do you have to these things? Was one a gift from a friend that you felt obligated to keep? Does the object stir up a recent memory? Find the emotional attachment.

Step three is about coming clean. By releasing these objects, you are making room in your life for more things to come. You are also freeing yourself from past memories that keep you in a place of lack. State in your journal why you think you can get rid of these items and how doing so will assist you emotionally.

Cleaning house is a great way to clear your mind. As you let go of material things, you also release your mind. Things that have been hanging around disappear and create new space. As you create space, you also create space inside yourself. This exercise gives you double the reward!

Lastly, make sure you follow through and get rid of these articles. Make notes in your journal about how it felt to do so. If they are objects you don't want to actually throw in the trash, perhaps there is someone you could give them to. Don't procrastinate and prolong the process. You could give something to a friend and share your story with them about how letting go of this item is of benefit to you. This will be a very moving experience.

Day Six—Chain Reactions

Label today's jounal entry: **One Thing Led to Another, Which Led to Another**. Today I want you to write about a chain reaction you have experienced. *It all began with _____ , which led to something, which then led to something or someone else.* Continue with this until you get to the end of your story.

This entry is designed to help you understand how everything is connected (as we talked about in detail in the Hidden Gems chapter). Note the moments where you let go or surrendered. These are the moments when the next segment of your chain reaction often falls into place, but we tend to overlook these amazing moments.

Recall one of these strings of events. Become aware of each piece in the chain—the events within the entire string. Some events of this chain reaction flowed effortlessly, and almost unknowingly, you glided from one occurrence to the next. You may find that you struggled with one event in the string, as if you came up against a wall. Perhaps you tried to push it out of the way, attempted to break it down, got frustrated with it, or even begged and pleaded it to change for you. You were fighting instead of gracefully going with the flow. You used blame, told someone off, or engaged "should have"/"shouldn't have" thoughts. Eventually, something about you softened. You're not done with it, and you just let it go. This is the moment when you connect with ease and joy and move to the next event in the string.

Your mission today is to reflect in your journal about one of the chain reactions in your life that led to a positive outcome.

Day Seven—A Little Bit of Heaven

Label today's jounal entry: **The Things I Work For.** Money is the ruler of us all—or so it seems. Wouldn't it be interesting if we worked for experience instead of money? Imagine going to work and receiving experiences instead of money. For example, this week you are working for the experience of redecorating your bedroom. The entire thing! You're choosing new furniture, paint, and the works. Next month, you are working for the experience of a month break in Tibet. You work each week or month for an experience. Maybe you worked for the experience of whitewater rafting or what it feels like to sit on top of a mountain? It could be the experience of being an author or a teacher. Don't get caught up in the reality of it; get caught up in the experience! Write about five experiences you are working for.

Day Eight—Greetings

Label today's jounal entry: **Greetings!** It's time to reach out, ladies. It's time to connect with people for no apparent reason other than "because." This is sort of a double exercise.

Part one involves making a list of as many possible ways you could greet someone you have never met before. This includes all possible ways you could say hello to a stranger. Do your best to get creative—and even ridiculous if you can. While you are writing examples in your journal, imagine different people you might be greeting. Remember that the people are strangers. Who serves you coffee? Where do you buy groceries? Where do you eat? Where do you get your gas? Where do you go for walks? Where do you ride your bike? Where do you work out?

Part two of this fun, silly entry is using as many of these greetings as you can in the next three days. I want you to go out of your way to greet people who are strangers with all the greetings on your list. No cheating allowed! You know the outcome of part one of this exercise, but don't allow this to stop you from writing down your ideas. Journaling should be engaging, fun, and helpful. The purpose of this exercise is to get you to reach out to others. Don't ask for help, barf on anyone, or complain—just say hello and make your day a little more upbeat. Go get your greeting juju flowing!

Keep a record of what you loved about this exercise. If you had a bad experience, don't record it. What appeared to be stinky to you may have influenced the recipient in a way you could not see. They may have gone home that night—and paid it forward. Honestly, you never know!

Day Nine—Happy Holiday

Label today's jounal entry: **Taking a Break**. For this fun entry, I want you to make up your own holiday! Goodness knows we all want more days where we can let go of work and enjoy more fun! To begin, name your holiday. Once you've named it, ask yourself why we need this holiday. Get those pens poised and start writing! Explain how it will be celebrated? Give details about the whole theme around it? Describe how it feels!

Mine would be Do Nothing Day. I think people need to play with the pleasure of doing less. We're always giving everything purpose. Too often, we chastise ourselves for doing nothing, telling ourselves we wasted a day. North Americans (if indeed you are from North America) would benefit from learning the art of just being—and being happy with that. You could sit outside and read a book, watch movies all day, take a long nap (or several naps through the day), lie in the sun, go for a walk, whatever. You just can't be productive today. That would be my day! I'm sure you will come up with an amazing day we all would love!

Day Ten—Who's That?

Label today's jounal entry: **Who's That?** Today is about getting in touch with your stress, but in a different way than continually letting it wreak havoc on your body. Let's play with the idea of taking your stress outside of yourself and giving it an identity. I want you to give it life!

Stress is like a nasty monster residing in the world of you. Let's give it a personality and a life, but don't worry about naming it. Take all your stress, pent-up anger, and frustration and create your Frankenstein. Get out your journal and start describing what it would look like. Imagine your stress is sitting in the room with you. Think about how your anxiety makes you feel, and do your best to visualize how it would look. Picture how it might be dressed. What colors and types of clothing might it wear? Describe its posture. What gestures does it use when it talks? Does it look old or young? Is it short or tall? Is it male or female? Describe some of its facial features. Does it look healthy or sick? What does its hair look like? How does it walk? What does its voice sound like? How do people react when it is near?

This quest will help you realize how ridiculous your stress is. You will see how monstrous it is—and how you are allowing such a thing to be in charge of you. Would you like to hang around this nasty thing every day? By giving your stress an identity outside of you, I am hoping you might free yourself from its grips a bit. In the future, when you feel this awful creature taking control, you will be able to detect it and put some separation between you and it.

Day Eleven—Brush It Off

Label today's jounal entry: **Who's Going to Know?** Julia Child said, "Always remember: If you are in the kitchen and you drop the lamb, you can always pick it up. Who's going to know?"

Look at situations or rules you take way too seriously. Like Julia said, no one is going to know if you drop the lamb. We protect ourselves, our integrity, and our values even when no one is watching by not allowing ourselves the opportunity to brush something off. Think of a situation you take too seriously—perhaps a rule you think exists that you believe you have to follow—and write about it. Your target is to attempt to break it down and learn how silly you are by always expecting the worst outcome. Maybe it's a superstition like lucky socks or not touching escalator handrails because the germs might attach themselves to you?

Once, while driving home very late at night, I came to a stoplight. On the outskirts of the city, especially at that time of the night, there was very little traffic. I pulled up, stopped, and waited to make a left turn. I waited and waited. I began to wonder why I was sitting there. Not a car was in sight—just silly me waiting for a traffic light to give me permission to turn left. How crazy is that? With the red stoplight beaming at me, I considered making my turn. All kinds of thoughts burst like bubbles in my head.

Catherine, you know it's wrong to run a red light! If you do, you are breaking the law. You will get caught. Only bad people would consider doing this. What if a cop is lurking somewhere, watching and waiting to pounce on someone just like you?

As that last thought flashed in my mind, I made my turn! I realized how silly this rule was in my particular circumstance, and I ignored it.

It's like throwing away a whole leg of lamb because you dropped it on the floor when you could have washed it off or waiting for a light to turn green at three in the morning when you are the only person in the vicinity. It's ridiculous! Write about something you could just brush off once in a while and not take so seriously.

Day Twelve—Mmm

Label today's jounal entry: **Smells I Love!** Today is all about the smells you love! Research has proven that smells can be triggers for almost anything—pain, romance, dreams, stress, you name it. Today, journal about all the scrumptious smells you love and how they make you feel.

I love to light candles every day and spray my bed with spicy scents. It makes climbing into bed a pure pleasure. Lavender is a scent I enjoy when I am meditating because it helps me relax. I love to smell Chester Pug! Yes—dog stink smells good to me. I used to tell my ex I could identify my pets by smelling them if I was blindfolded. I have a very strong sense of smell; I can even smell ozone levels rising and dropping in the air.

Get in touch with some of the smells you love. Choose the ones that make you feel relaxed and happy. What scents do you enjoy in a room or on your body? Even if you are sensitive, don't cop out and say you don't like smells. Do you like the smell of coffee or cookies baking? Do you love the way your clothes smell right out of the dryer? When I smell certain types of plastic, I'm reminded of the very first doll I received so many Christmases ago! Do you like floral, woody, natural, citrus, or spicy smells? Get into some sniffing action, identify some smells you love, and write all about them.

Day Thirteen—My Own Space

Label today's jounal entry: **Solitude versus Loneliness**. In this journal entry, compare the differences between these two words—and turn some of your loneliness into solitude. Define these two similar words in your own way and decide where you fit with them. Look at this time alone with yourself from a different perspective. Come up with ways to transform some of your loneliness into solitude. Take this one slowly. Give yourself some space and time to think. This is a bit more challenging, but it is very rewarding!

Day Fourteen—Future Thinking

Label today's jounal entry: **I Remember When**. In this last journal entry, imagine you have advanced into the future and are now the lovely age of eighty. Okay, there are some rules to this game. Remember that we are only thinking positively here. You are not to assume you are old, frail, crippled, or dying! Picture yourself as a vibrant, active eighty-year-old woman who has overcome all the stuff you are struggling with right now. You are living a very happy, loving, prosperous life. Picture this scene as best you can.

You are happy, healthy, and youthful. As you stand in front of the hall mirror, putting on your jacket in preparation for an event being held in your honor, you see a vision a younger version of yourself. Memories of the turmoil you encountered at that time in your life come flooding back to you as you look into the eyes of this younger you. You stare at each other and finally say hello; the younger you says hello too.

This is your opportunity to tell the younger version of you an inspiring story of how life went in your favor. Encourage her. Let her know that everything turned out just fine. Write from the perspective of the older version of you. Help the younger you relax and go with the flow. Show her how important she is. How creative. How loving. How magical life will be for her! Give her hope. Give her encouragement. Give her you!

I hope these exercises helped you get in the swing of using a journal. Many people think keeping a journal is writing about what happened that day, how we feel about what's going on in our lives, disclosing who was mean to us, or what we don't like. But it doesn't have to be. Journaling can be a boost to your spirit. It can be a fun, creative experience that gives you the opportunity to consider what you have never considered before. Once you are on a roll, you can continue on your own. If you enjoyed a few specific days in particular, use the topics as many times as you like. Repeating them will only be to your benefit. Journaling can change your life if you let it. Don't be afraid. Go online and search for other topics to journal about or come up with a few of your own. If you would like to share them with others on my website, please e-mail me at meandmypassions@gmail.com.

These exercises are intended to encourage you and provide an understanding of the many opportunities in front of you. We often get stuck in one way of thinking, which makes it difficult to see the many forks in the road. There are forks jutting out all the time—you simply don't see them with your eyes. Each fork is an option you can choose.

Sometimes you make choices out of fear—and have a rough experience. Sometimes you listen to your intuition—and the result is an easier path. Have you ever ignored a very strong urge to do something that ended in a way that wasn't what you had hoped for? You might have the same urge later, give into it, and watch everything change for the better. Those are forks.

Life would be crazy if we were able to see every single alternative available to us. We wouldn't know where to begin. It's so much more fun when you don't know what's ahead. That's why it's good to get in touch with how you feel in all situations. When you know how you feel, you know whether something feels good or not when opportunities present themselves. That is when you are able to choose what's best for you. You learn how not to settle because you don't think there is another alternative. Many of us think there is only one option. If we turn one opportunity down, we don't believe that another will come along. It's true that there is more than one way to skin a cat.

You're at one of those forks now. You've made a series of choices, and you have selected paths that have led you to where you are right now. Don't fall into the trap of trying to figure out what possibilities you might have turned down. Instead, understand that if something doesn't feel good to you when it shows up, then it isn't good. From where you are right now, be open to the ideas that pop up.

Perhaps a guy will say hi to you today, and you will freak out because you are not willing to get involved with anyone. This guy could be a whole different experience for you. He could be an opportunity knocking, helping you decide what you are ready for and when. He could just be a guy saying hi. Does he fill another need in your life? He could be a business owner looking for someone with your skills or the connecting person that leads you to something else. Open up and stay on the lookout. Pay attention to your gut when stuff falls into your lap—and all will be fine.

Chapter Eleven
IT'S YOU AND ONLY YOU. IS THAT A PROBLEM?

Take a look at the space you live in. Does it feel like you or someone else? It should be all about you—and only you—in this space (kids or not). What you choose to surround yourself with should be a reflection of you now—not you then.

When I moved out, homeowner duties did not appeal to me moving forward on my own. Did you choose to stay? Are you now living in the home that you and your ex purchased and possibly raised your children in? How much of your ex is still in this place? Part of redefining and finding yourself requires creating an atmosphere that feels like you. Reorganizing and redecorating helps the reinventing process. If you are in your marital home, this doesn't mean you have to overhaul the entire place! Create a living area that reflects you instead of the compromise you gave into because of a difference in tastes. If you moved to a new home, this is your opportunity to create a space that reflects who you really are.

A lot of women played the role of chief decorator in their marital homes. Most of the decor in your home may already suit you more than it did your ex. Take a look around anyway. Does this feel more like *us* rather than *me*? Would some reorganization help—maybe a few more feminine touches splashed around?

Let's start with your bedroom. There is no better room to splash yourself around in than your boudoir. Separation or divorce makes most women question their desirability. All too often, we choose to decorate our bedrooms in a way that is also pleasing to the men in our lives, but it's time for a change. Let's redecorate this room for the new you! Now is the time to reclaim your space, and a bedroom is one of the best places to augment your own unique feminine vibe!

Are you on the prowl for a new lover—or have you sworn off men for a while? If pink and flowery is your style, and you have never been able to express it in the bedroom, it is sure to repel any man from wanting to spend much time in there with you. If this is your goal, you go, girl! You can also choose to make your room feminine—and not repel men. In fact, you can lure them in with seductive colors, scents, and plush pillows. After all, men have a feminine side too! It doesn't matter what you choose—as long as it makes you feel good.

Calling Your Inner Diva

Take a serious look at this space. How does it look and feel? Walk outside the room and take a deep breath. Let's play a little game again. You may not utilize your inner diva, but you are about to. This inner vixen knows exactly what she finds sexy, sultry, sassy, and seductive. Let's call her out. Take another long, deep breath. As you draw air deep into your lungs, embody your inner diva. As you breathe out, let her completely take over.

This exercise may sound silly, and some of you might say I'm asking you to create and put on another a mask. This is not the case. This exercise will help you call on character traits that are a part of you—but you may keep them hidden. You are fully aware of the power this inner sister has. She is part of who you are.

Let's play with this diva part of you by being fully conscious and aware that you are doing so. A mask is something you create subconsciously out of need. This is play, and you are fully aware. Okay, go! Embody your inner diva and walk back into your bedroom:

- What about this room doesn't feel like me?
- What simply has to go because it's my ex's?
- What colors would be yummy in here?
- What's my style?

What came up? Perhaps the furniture is too masculine, the colors are too bland, or there is nothing remotely frilly or feminine about the space. Don't go into panic mode and think you need to purchase all new furniture—unless you really want to and can afford that expense. Imagine some of the details that would help you redecorate your bedroom with your own unique feminine touches. Turn this old drab marital bedroom upside down.

If this is a new space, and not your marital bedroom, play with this exercise in exactly the same way. What shade would be yummy on the walls that your practical ex would have vetoed? What colors appeal to your inner diva? Think about your personality. Are you a sports girl or are you into chick flicks? Pastel colors and luxurious linens may be a better reflection of ladies who are brought to tears by a sappy movie. More masculine gals may enjoy deeper, neutral shades with a pop of color.

Consider the shapes you like. My friends say I'm a circle girl. I love curvy lines and circular shapes. I do not like furniture lined up and in order. My living room is always set up on an angle, and I rearrange my furniture regularly. It also features different shaped articles and with a tree decal on one wall with big round blossoms in green and silver. The walls are dotted with my own artwork, which is a reflection of the curvy, sexy me.

Your body shape can help you choose a style that is linear or circular. This may sound strange, but the shape of your body is often what you project onto your surroundings. My body is curvy, and I enjoy adding those curves to the spaces I live in. I love big puffy pillows with wild textures, circular objects, flowers, and candles. I balance this with contemporary furniture. If you are tall and thin, squares and rectangles may appeal more to you.

Make it your mission to remove anything that feels too much like your ex. Did he demand a television in the room? Is this something you desire in this space? If not, move it out. This is often a topic of great debate when redecorating a bedroom. You may love having a television in your bedroom to relax and watch, but other women would say the bedroom is not a place for a television. I am in the latter group. Although I have often thought it would be nice to watch a movie in bed, it is not a piece of furniture I want in my bedroom.

Think sex, sex, and sex ... even if it's the furthest idea from your mind. This area is a reflection of you and how sexy you are—even if you don't feel sexy at this moment. The whole reason for picking up this book is because you have a desire to redefine yourself.

What can you create in this space? I find strong, rich colors, such as purple or brown, depict sexiness better than red does. How about choosing low-light options to really create a romantic ambience? Scents, plants, color, and lighting bring their own drama to a bedroom. I love burning candles at night while I read or write in bed.

This is your haven, a place to relax and unwind. Your surroundings should make you happy. It's you and only you—for now. This exercise will help you become comfortable with this. Your outlook on life is changing. You are beginning to remember all that you really love to do, which you have set aside for far too long. You are writing from your heart and remembering who you are. You are letting go of people who no longer benefit your personal growth. You are reclaiming your space and making it your own. Imagine arriving home—to your own space. You are moving forward. Have some fun with your bedroom. Let it seep out into your living room, and so on, and so on.

Chapter Twelve
BRAG YOUR LITTLE HEART OUT

I talk a lot with my clients about the words they use to talk about themselves. Most people have a difficult time talking positively and sharing their greatness. Many of us were taught by our parents or caregivers to practice being humble and quiet about our skills and talents. Unfortunately, choosing to keep these great features about who we are hidden—and keeping ourselves small—causes us a great deal of stress when we are asked to share a list of positive qualities about ourselves. It doesn't feel natural to acknowledge our greatness in any way. We've bought into the belief that bragging makes us sound conceited.

Part of the belief that it is not acceptable to talk about our accomplishments involves the idea that we may offend others in doing so. With this viewpoint that bragging is an undesirable quality, something as common as a job interview becomes overwhelming. Employers expect us to promote ourselves to them as confident go-getters, but we've never been taught to do so. A system that primarily encompasses a method of evaluation that focuses on our weaknesses and the qualities and skills someone else thinks we need to develop makes it challenging for people to embrace the idea that they have amazing strengths and abilities. It's right back to keeping us small and in control.

We have become so entrenched in this humble way of thinking that we gladly announce our weaknesses. We create from lack —instead of abundance. We are a society of people who see ourselves as broken, often unfixable, rather than acknowledging the geniuses we really are.

Do you know how rare it is to hear someone say they are talented, unless they have been told so over and over again? If we do praise ourselves, we might say, "Well, I've been told I make a pretty good apple pie!" The truth is that your apple pies are probably out of this world! People could be lined up down the street and around the corner to sample your yummy apple pie, but you would do your best to remain unnoticed, small, and insignificant.

We simply can't pat ourselves on our backs and admit that we have extraordinary qualities and talents. We believe everyone else is better than we are; at the same time, everyone else has the same opinion of themselves as we do. Struggle is the way to get the best stuff, right? Sharing what we enjoy doing is acceptable, but we rarely brag about how fantastic we are at anything. How many years have you put into you so far? I've put a good forty-eight years into exposing the real me; why shouldn't I be proud of what I have created? Why shouldn't you? Why shouldn't everyone?

People today are also expected to fit many more roles in their careers. In Western society, it has become common practice for employees to be required to have a broader range of skills than specialize in only one. The Internet has become a driver of everything from shopping to booking your seats at the movie theater. People are communicating in ways they never used to. In a time where workdays are becoming longer—and workloads are exploding to the point where most of us can't keep up—a common complaint is that many of us do not feel acknowledged for what we do and that we are overworked and overwhelmed.

I have always seen myself as someone who keeps fairly up to date with technology, but the energies today are moving very fast! Do you feel like a relic at work? I can't tell you how many of my clients struggle in their work environments. What does any of this have to do with how you talk about yourself? Constantly being reminded that your skills and knowledge are behind the times makes it more difficult for you to acknowledge your unique qualities.

A friend of mine was going for a job interview. She was worried about the whole experience, as most people are. I encouraged her to relax and breathe and know that everything would work out perfectly.

She said, "I hate interviews! I don't like having to go into a room with someone I don't know and market myself to them, knowing they are comparing me to a ton of other applicants expected to do the same!"

Her comments made me think about bragging and how valuable it would be for us to learn how to brag in a way that wasn't considered putting anyone else down or didn't come off as being conceited. Imagine if we were all confident in our skills and abilities and were able to express them out loud?

Being a single woman again has opened my eyes about how impossible living on your own can be if you cannot see all your own great qualities. If you can't connect with yourself, who else is going to want to associate with you? Be that which you want to attract.

I'm going to ask you a question. When you read it, stop for three minutes (which will seem like an eternity, but play with me) and write down whatever comes to mind in your journal. You can do this!

Here is the big question. If you and I were just introduced, and I asked you to tell me about yourself, what would you share with me about who you are?

Get out your journal and give me your explanation of you.

The clock is ticking, ticking, ticking

Write your answer.

Who are you?

What can you tell me, a total stranger, about you?

The clock is still ticking.

Don't give up. Just answer the question.

Hi. My name is ...

I am ...

How are you doing?

Come up with any good stuff?

Almost done?

Okay, three minutes is up! Now, let's see what you came up with. Tick off any of the below statements you listed about yourself:

☐   Your name
☐   Your age
☐   Your job or what you do for a living

- ☐ A bit of a brag about your career and how well you do it
- ☐ How long you've worked in this position or with this company
- ☐ Your marital status
- ☐ What city you live in
- ☐ Something nasty about the break up with your ex or how it is affecting you right now
- ☐ The fact that you have been through a terrible, life-altering event
- ☐ The kind of music you like
- ☐ Something you are struggling with
- ☐ How many children you have
- ☐ Something about the way you look
- ☐ How you hate talking about yourself

How many of those did you tick off? When I ask my clients this question, most responses include information similar to what I have listed above. It's unbelievable how we have such a narrow way of defining ourselves, only including the surface details to describe us—and only a sprinkling of who we really are.

This is how we have been taught to exchange pleasantries with strangers. This constricted list provides nothing personal. When chatting with someone we have just met, we will talk about our children, where we work, what we do to pay our bills, whether we like our jobs, where we went to school, and even where we were born and raised—but nothing truly personal. In fact, if we do boast about our accomplishments, it will be to an outsider and not someone we already know. We have an easier time bragging to a stranger than we do bragging to people we know.

The things that pump us up and get our blood flowing are the secrets we keep folded in our back pockets, only sharing them with those who first reveal something similar from *their* secret list.

We share our secrets with a select few we feel a connection with. We don't see our passions as important—or we think they are so important we must keep them hidden in an effort to safeguard our inner self. We only share our accomplishments publicly. We boast about the courses we have taken, which college or university we attended, the assortment of letters we have accumulated behind our name, how hard we work and how little we play, the types of people we surround ourselves with (who we know), how big a home we own (the area we live in), and the types of toys we have collected (our societal category). We have been taught that this is acceptable information to share openly.

We are very skilled at leaving who we really are out of the equation and squeezing ourselves into someone else's definition of importance. This was the primary struggle I encountered with the first man I dated. Early in our relationship, it became apparent that I had actually put myself below him instead of equal with him. We had extensive conversations where he spoke of his accomplishments, and I shared my desires to empower individuals and build an organization where we would stimulate self-love, expand consciousness, and do business differently. Together we played the game of appearing interested in each other's points of view, but my preferences and beliefs soon became topics of doubt to him. When I did talk about my passions, I found myself defending them—not sharing them lovingly. We generally agreed to disagree. Of course, this made me think he was not interested in my desires, and I clammed up and made myself small.

I am very proud of who I have become—as you should be too. I've crafted myself perfectly. There is much I have released in order to discover and embrace new, positive possibilities. I love the choices I have made—and where they have led me. I found it interesting that I had chosen a relationship with a man who supported the types of limiting points of view I had released.

It was not my intention to change his way of thinking to mimic my own. I had no desire to make him think he was wrong or that my perspectives were right, but I was aware that I had attracted the same tones in a man as I had in many past relationships. They were the tones of limitation, restriction, disempowerment, and control that dotted my past. That was what I had become accustomed to receiving. With this clear realization, I should have ended the relationship. Instead, I chose to cut off pieces of myself so I could fit into his world in order to feel accepted. I chose to be less of me—and stayed in a limiting relationship—because I was afraid of being alone. I wanted to be loved again.

It's not about looking in the mirror at yourself; it is about feeling and exposing more of yourself.

This book is all about you. My goal has been to help you dig deep and rediscover more of who you are. Now I would like you to express on paper—and out loud—all the wonderful attributes and qualities you keep hidden on your private list. It's not about looking in the mirror at yourself; it is about feeling and exposing more of you. Deep inside, we all know we have gifts to share, but it's so darn difficult to say them out loud. We choose not to love, trust, or share ourselves. In relationships, we almost snap when we don't understand why the other person doesn't *know us*. We bury the special qualities we admire in ourselves because society has led us to believe that bragging is not acceptable.

You can't tell me you don't have any good qualities. If I were to ask you to talk about your weaknesses, you would babble on until I stopped you! Why have you decided that point of view is acceptable? We talk about greatness, but we don't fully believe in it—or expect it from ourselves. We are afraid of our own power. We are afraid to be hurt or exposed. We've been taught it's better to be poor than to be powerful. Who do you think came up with this way of thinking in the first place? Is it more beneficial to be the prison guard or the prisoner?

The only way we seem able to accept bragging is for the benefit of self-promotion and public speaking. Selling yourself includes sharing the benefits of utilizing your skills with others. Why isn't it acceptable to brag about our passions openly? There is so much remarkable information about you that you keep hidden.

Business coaches teach that self-promotion is an asset. The elevator speech they teach is a brief summary that quickly describes a product, service, or organization and its value proposition. Unfortunately, this concept has been adopted as a way of introducing ourselves in social settings. Do you honestly believe you can be summed up in less than three minutes? I think not! I say shout it out for as long as you can! Gee—only three minutes to express all of your greatness! Goodness knows, if you talk for too long about yourself, someone might think you feel superior. We wouldn't want anyone to feel bad because you're proud of yourself, would we?

When I talk of bragging, it's not about one-upping anyone. That is not my definition of bragging, although it has been linked to bragging. One-upping is done with the purpose of making others feel bad; it involves boosting our own ego, and ego loves it! The problem with bragging has more to do with the word itself. It's another word that has been given a really bad rap. It would be of much more value to everyone if we redefined this word in a more effective manner.

I adore redefining words—and making up new ones! Who cares how some silly book defines it? I think it's best to redefine a word if it doesn't work for you. It's about time that bragging was redefined—and all the extra baggage it includes dumped. So let's do it!

Bragging: Speaking with excessive pride about an achievement or possession.

Okay, this not all bad. In fact, I quite like this definition—except for the *excessive* part. We've all experienced someone who has dominated a conversation. Excessive exaggeration or dominating conversations takes things to a whole other level—and angers people.

When we talk about ourselves, most would agree that there are restrictions to what we can boast about. Why do we agree to limit ourselves according to someone else's standards? What if my interpretation of what is acceptable boasting is different than other people's definitions? Wouldn't it be marvelous if everyone bragged about their passions instead of just their achievements and possessions? How about sharing our talents—or anything we know we are pretty darn good at?

Imagine having a conversation with three other women where one asks what's been going on in your world. It would feel incredible to say, "Thanks for asking! I recently facilitated an amazing TeleWebSeries with some outstanding speakers on anchoring prosperity. It was absolutely delicious!"

This is not the typical response. Most people say, "Oh, fine, fine. I'm doing well. How about you?"

Can you feel the lack of electricity in this response compared to the first one?

Bragging 101

The trick to bragging is sharing something juicy—and then shutting up. This gives others the opportunity to ask you to share more about what you have stated—or not. It gives them a choice. This approach sets you up to receive. It's so much tastier! Try it.

"Hey Catherine, what's been going on in your world?"

"Thanks for asking! I recently facilitated an amazing TeleWebSeries with some outstanding speakers on anchoring prosperity. It was absolutely delicious!"

"That sure sounds interesting. What is a TeleWebSeries?"

"Have you never attended a TeleWebSeries? They are often called telesummits and are free telecasts you participate in and listen to online or by phone. They can be on any topic—from prosperity, relationships, business coaching, body image, abundance and money, or even health."

This is where we usually go astray and dominate the conversation. The secret to this technique is to continue to provide bite-sized yummy bits of information that entice listeners to keep asking for more. You can also hand the conversation over to someone else at any time, which gives the impression of being humble.

You could say, "I'm sure someone here attended an online telecall or telesummit." This will motivate others to join in this fun, positive, bragging conversation.

What you share does not have to be about business—or anything you would normally define as significant. You could say, "Thanks for asking! I just made the most delicious pies this past weekend."

You could also say, "Lately I have been into reading and devouring book after book."

Can you see how fun bragging can be—and how building your bragging skills can be fun for others too?

Brag: A boastful announcement or display of arrogant behavior.

This sounds pretty nasty, but boasting isn't all bad. It's just overemphasizing something. This is not to be confused with exaggerating, which blows up everything far too big for it to be believable. The kicker here is in the word "arrogant." Arrogance doesn't work for most of us because it is all about showing contempt for others or disregarding them. Not so nice! If we were to boast in a way similar to the examples I have provided, people would be subject to receiving and sharing more juicy things.

This isn't a big deal; it's an easy one to redefine. I'm creating my own definition.

Bragging:

Boasting joyfully to others with pride regarding our passions, inborn and learned skills, and achievements with the intention of sharing our good nature. Speaking openly about the wonderful, unique traits of who we really are. Expressing our strengths with the sole purpose of feeling good while encouraging others to step into their own power and feel good too.

With this definition, bragging isn't all bad. Bragging is another fantastic journal exercise to try. Back away from the encyclopedia, grab some of your personal power, and let some good stuff spurt out of you! Better yet, share this new definition of bragging with someone close to you and practice bragging to each other. We brag in my classes all the time. In fact, one whole class is dedicted to bragging. It can be difficult at first, but once you catch on, it's extremely empowering and fun!

Why is talking negatively more acceptable than bragging?

Bragging should never be done with the desire to push anyone away from you; it should encourage them and bring them closer. Would people want to listen to you if all you did was barf negativity onto them? Of course not. So why is talking negatively more acceptable than bragging? Why do we openly share the crap going on in our life—and keep the good stuff a secret? Do you continually encourage self-abuse by keeping yourself small and playing down your strengths? It is time to leave the barf parties behind!

Get out your journal and label this journal entry "Bragging My Heart Out for the Very First Time—and Loving It!" Record the new definition of bragging that I shared earlier. Write, "What's been going on with you lately?" in your journal, and start bragging to the world about all of the wonderful, fun things you are creating and experiencing in your life. When you get stuck, refer to the definition or the previous examples. Brag about yourself in your journal for as long as you can.

Another fun exercise for getting in touch with your wonderful qualities uses your name. Use each letter of your name to state something positive about yourself.

My Example Name Brag

My name is Catherine. This stands for Courageous—Attractive—Tell it Like it Is—Has to Have the Last Word—Energy Healer—Richer than I Can Imagine—Imperfect and Loving it—Nothing is Impossible—Evolving. *Catherine.*

Or how about going on your own bragging rampage?

My Example Brag Rampage

I'm passionate about living my passions. I love inspiring others to embody self-love and explore themselves on deeper levels. I'm a people watcher and an analyzer. Sitting at the beach is as much a delight to my mind as it is to my senses.

People amaze and inspire me. There is nothing finer than watching someone morph a negative situation into a positive one—with the realization that the answers came from within. This is empowering for me.

I adore having a lot of friends, but I love time to myself. Painting, scrapbooking, and creative things are fun for me. I'm a writer and an author.

My body is sexy and curvy and aging perfectly! My hair is white, and I have fun making it whatever color I choose. I've made friends and enemies, and I've learned from both. I'm single and loving it because I get to call all the shots. I love to hog the bed, smell the fresh air, listen to the sounds the leaves make when the wind blows, and I can't list a favorite food because there are too many I love to choose only one.

I stay as far away from the news and media as possible, and I have a very open, eclectic belief system. I find the smell of a campfire intoxicating, although camping is one of my least favorite activities. Some of my favorite things are red wine, a good hand massage, a ritzy hotel room, a man's hands, spicy candle scents, writing, painting, watching movies, and snuggling with Chester Pug.

Wow—that felt good! Now it's your turn. My example gives you an idea of how far I want you to take this. Once you get your groove on, you should start to feel as if you've been given a boost of energy. It immediately feels good because it's *your* truth. You know what you like, but you don't think about it. You probably think about the opposite of what you like, which makes you feel disconnected from the things you know you love. It's about disclosing some of the little secrets you usually keep under wraps. Sharing these little details—the mini electrifying pieces of you—can offer someone else a whole new perspective of who you are.

Some people like to start a brag book. A few times a week, they devote time to brag and keep that boost energized. It's entirely up to you how you choose to brag. I know this may sound like a weird practice, but it helps you rediscover and reinvent *you*.

Many people say, "You just have to love yourself or no one else will."

That's a nice statement, but how the heck do you instantly love yourself if you haven't up until now? It's like trying to get someone who is depressed to suddenly be happy. It's not going to happen overnight. This is why I have shared the little tricks I work and play with. Indulge in more play and transform how you think about yourself. The transformation is the fun part! Stop trying to rush things. Bragging is about expressing your own personal truth—without any masks. It's like building a large bubble inside of yourself that gets bigger and bigger and bursts out of you.

The Real Deal

Here is the real deal about bragging. People don't like hearing about other people's accomplishments or the good going on in their lives because they are jealous. Jealousy has been given a bad rap too. Jealousy is a sign you send yourself to indicate that you are not being true to your passions. Pay attention. People compare their current situations to the pretty picture you painted—and they don't like it. We all have our own pretty pictures going on, but we usually don't bother to see them this way.

People also take everything too personally. For some reason, we think a person sharing wonderful news about their lives is slighting us in some way. If I told you that my son did not need to attend preschool because he was advanced and already knew everything he would learn from doing so—and your daughter was struggling in preschool—how would my story make you feel?

If you took what I said personally, you might think thoughts like, *She knows my daughter is struggling in preschool. Why would she say such a thing to me? Why is she being so cruel?*

You could be upset because you do not think it is nice to brag about a situation you are struggling with. My comments would feel like a personal attack because you have your own thing going on with how you feel about her daughter's situation. This is a common reaction for most of us.

Can you imagine not being able to share anything good in your life because you were afraid of being judged as uncaring, arrogant, or rude? Imagine always being consciously aware of everyone else's situations—and only speaking about topics everyone can agree on. That would be crazy. If I meet a man and feel wonderful, am I not to share this joyous news with any woman because she might be unhappy in her marriage or lonely? Do you see how absurd this sounds? What if a friend publishes a book and receives a huge amount of money, but my book is rejected by the major publishers? Should she not share her happiness with me? If I married a rich man who gave me trinkets and took me on trips around the world, should I not share this because someone may have lost their job?

Do you see how silly we have become about bragging? We have made it the norm not to share joy because we are afraid that we will be judged as uncaring individuals who are out to make other people feel inferior.

Walt Whitman said, "If you done it, it ain't bragging." I tend to agree with him. We should be proud of everything we have done. Bragging takes a nasty twist when it is someone's desire to put down someone else in order to feel better about who they are. As long as your objective is to share something wonderful, all is good. How other people choose to interpret what you are saying depends wholly upon their own state of mind.

As a single, forty-plus woman, you need to talk about your passions to keep your spirits high and boost your confidence. Most women, after separation or divorce, don't brag ... they barf. If they are bragging, it's mostly about all the stuff they pilfered from the divorce! If this is your story, I would recommend letting go of it.

Get out there and practice bragging. Think of something positive to communicate with a close friend. Maybe it's a scoopy deal you found on a new pair of shoes or a free Internet stick for your computer you received when you purchased your new phone. Get a little more personal and share a great weekend story. Start with small brags—and always make it your intention to share something wonderful.

Chapter Thirteen
THE MAN FACTOR

All across the globe, thousands of women over forty are experiencing being single for the first time in years and are adjusting to a new way of living. Some love their newfound freedom, and others desire to explore dating or casual sex. A vast majority are simply undecided.

On a delicious summer afternoon, a friend and I toddled off to the beach to soak up some sun. While digging our toes into the sand and relaxing in the sun, I could not help but eavesdrop on an intimate encounter between a two lovers near the shore. The man came jogging out of the water and lovingly tossed himself onto his lover, forcing her back onto the sand. It was quite obvious he was not preoccupied with how onlookers viewed such a public display of affection, as he smothered her with kisses. The woman glowed as she received his affections.

I could not help but want to take her place and experience being gifted so much love. The smile on her face said it all. I was instantly jealous. I was suddenly aware of how strong the desire was within me to enjoy my life with a man in this way. Being on your own can be a bit of a drag sometimes, but I have spent many days lounging around till noon—with no one nagging me about how unproductive I was being.

One afternoon, I met with a few friends I hadn't seen in ages. We had a wonderful time chatting about our life adventures: our kids and how kooky they are sometimes, everything we don't have the time or energy to bother doing, our jobs and how bad they are, how much weight we've lost or gained since last together. I shared my writing experience, and my girlfriend talked about her adventures transforming an old church into a restaurant. We released this woman energy and went our separate ways.

On my ride up the elevator to my apartment, I was joined by another tenant. Before the elevator began its ascent, she asked me which floor my apartment was on.

"The eighth," I answered. "Up in the corner with a fantastic view of the city!"

I love living in a high-rise apartment. The views are stunning.

Chuckling, she divulged that she was in the same apartment on a lower level. "I remember saying once that my dream house would be facing northeast and would overlook a body of water. Well, I got exactly what I asked for, didn't I?" I looked at her a bit puzzled, and she continued, "I'm in a northeast-facing apartment with a great view overlooking a body of water ... a pool!"

We both laughed as the elevator arrived at her floor. As she stepped off, I began to wonder how many other single women must be arriving home alone.

In my apartment I was greeted by Chester Pug. He was bouncy and wanted kisses and cuddles; he made sure I received my fair share of loving from him. I relaxed on the sofa in my quiet apartment. It had been an excellent single woman day—the kind many married women crave. I was also aware of how being on my own could feel empty and disconnected.

My brilliant spirit stirred up memories to help ease my loneliness, soothing me with visions of my apartment filled with friends and joyful conversations. However, these loving memories were interrupted as my ego took over, conjuring twisted visions that bubbled up as fears. I felt extremely grateful for my doggy friend. Focusing my attention on him prevented the disturbing feelings from taking hold of me. Being on my own that day made me wonder if this was really what the rest of my life was going to be like.

Times like that can lead us to pondering the idea of having a partner in our lives again. Feelings of loneliness and insecurity provoke us to go on the prowl for the next Mr. Right. We daydream about being with a loving partner. We begin to feel a tug to find someone who really wants to be with us, make love, and create an exciting future together. A partner could enjoy exploring life, creating, and generating experiences and adventures outside of the ordinary working lifestyle. Lonely times often make us long for a man.

Seeking out a new partner during these isolated times is not in our best interests, but it is often our primary motivator. We are inherently driven to reach for what makes us feel good. We finally realize what we had when something is missing. Even if what we had was rotten, we find ourselves recalling all the good in it—and forgetting how it ended. We feel sorry for ourselves and initiate the search for a substitute for loneliness. We started the vicious circle by leaving a man—and now we are considering bringing a man back into our lives.

Ladies Like to Share

I enjoy how easily women share points of view and past experiences about topics of the heart. Men typically don't get this about us. Effortlessly, we slip into conversations about relationships, past and present, especially when the participants are of different generations or marital statuses. When younger women are involved in the conversation, it's all we can do to sustain ourselves from handing out free advice. You can almost picture us rubbing our hands together gleefully, waiting to pounce on the new little lovelies and setting them straight with all our relationship knowledge.

I recently had a conversation with a group of women much like this. *Zap!* Suddenly we were talking about relationships.

The eldest of the group said, "You just have to get that first marriage out of the way because the second one is so much better!"

Some heads bobbed in agreement, and others exhibited looks of puzzlement.

When asked why she felt this way, she replied, "Because the second time around, you just know what you want in a man. You also know what not to do in the relationship because you've learned from the stupid mistakes you made in the first one."

I laughed and nodded; I understood her point completely. She had pointed out one of the hidden gems that reveals itself long after the breakup. When a couple enters a marriage, they each have their own set of expectations and desires regarding how everything should play out. As we grow and mature, our desires do too. The relationships we nurture in our twenties don't always fit us in our thirties or forties. Our expectations change. In the same way we suddenly desire to change our hairstyle or try a new recipe, we decide sampling something new might be enjoyable, and we give it a go. She was saying that we change. We learn from our experiences—whether they brought us joy or sorrow. From these, we create new expectations and desires. We learn. We evolve. We make new discoveries about who we are.

One of the hidden gems I learned from my marriage was to not try to change a man in any way to make me happy. Unfortunately, changing a man is something women joke about all too often. We make snide comments about molding a man into what we want him to be. It's no joke—we are quite serious. I came to my own realization that this was a silly way of living. How could anyone ever feel good about themselves if they were living in order to make me happy? To do so, they would have to ignore many of their own desires.

You have an underlying list of deal breakers and must-have mate characteristics.

Even if you don't pursue a relationship for quite some time—or ever again—it is a good idea to be aware of your deal breakers and must-have characteristics. There should never be an actual list—as it's ever changing—but we all have a subconscious one.

We pull from this subconscious list and sum up a guy on the first date. We notice his eating habits, the way he's dressed, how thoughtful he is, grooming habits, his car, his job, where he lives, how he spends his free time, how much free time he actually has, and any words he uses that are emotional triggers from our past relationships.

Many people say, "You will never find a person who will fit all of the things on your list. That's just impossible."

That may be so, but it's still important to know what qualities about your former mate you were ready to release—and what sort of characteristics you can easily overlook.

Do you have any idea how many women let a man slip away due to some silly quality they believe they can't live with? Do you hate when your guy constantly watches sports programs, or that he barges in the bathroom while you are taking a pee, how he shifts his balls in his pants during a deep conversation with you, or how he is louder in public than you think is reasonable? Does he have a distinctive laugh or flamboyant gestures? We draw these little character tidbits of information from our subconscious—without even knowing we are doing so—and draw conclusions.

Did you know that each of these tidbits of information corresponds to networks of neurons in your brain, which has connections that increase with each repeated experience? Every time you experience or learn something, the neural circuits are altered in your brain. Each time you repeat them, they strengthen, forming pathways you draw upon when you experience something similar. A familiar laugh triggers a pathway in your brain. You relate the new experience to an old one, and you decide whether the past experience was pleasant and judge the new experience from this stored information. You relate the two circumstances and view them as the same.

What if you could consider each person you met without judgment? What if you let go of these patterns when you felt them surfacing and chose to understand that they are not related? How would this change your outlook on men—or anyone for that matter?

For many women who are "enjoying" singledom after forty, another marriage or even the thought of engaging in a casual relationship feels like inviting a scorpion to dinner. We pretend to enjoy his company, all the while expecting the stinger dangling behind his back to strike us between the eyes. It's those old neural pathways at work again.

Our memories of men are created out of experiences from our most recent relationships. We instinctively engage them—much the way we take the same route to get from one place to another—because of familiarity. In most cases, these relationships ended in heartbreak, and we can't release ourselves from our ties to these unpleasant thoughts. It is cumbersome to embrace new relationships with a fresh perspective, which causes us to assume the worst with new suitors. Women approach the "man factor" in different ways, depending on how often we engage the negative thoughts. It can be a challenge to let go of something when you continually give it your attention—whether you are doing so consciously or unconsciously.

We look at men and sum them up in a glance, expecting them not to be any different than the men from our past. It's not difficult to see why some women have no intention of pursuing any type of relationship with men for quite some time. They've closed one door and plan to keep it closed for the time being. They are not willing to connect emotionally. *It's too much work!* Maybe they've regained the control of their lives they gave away long ago. They may enjoy not having to justify every action and feel good about making decisions without the need for approval.

Is the fear of attracting another disastrous relationship overwhelming? Are your neural pathways working overtime?

We are a deeper,
richer brew now.

In the beginning of this newfound singledom, there is a need to regroup and remember who we are without the distraction of nurturing a new relationship. In this brewing time, we let the true flavors and essence of who we are come to the surface again. We are a deeper, richer brew now.

We are not only mothers or wives. We cannot be defined strictly by our career choices—nor by our past choices. Secretly we are writers, speakers, coaches, artists, historians, fashionistas, animal lovers, photographers, researchers, shamans, gossip columnists, dancers, activists, gardeners, counselors, organizers, decorators, astronomers, movie critics, musicians, hikers, people watchers, power walkers, bird watchers, designers, crafters, or collectors; the list of passions goes on and on.

One of my passions is people watching. I can sit for hours in a public place, observing people interacting. In a group setting, I enjoy picking up on everyone's vibe, giving me an overall feel for the energy in the room. Sitting quietly on the sidelines and evaluating people is not a practice looked upon positively. I was generally thought of as being not much of a conversationalist, but all the while I was checking people out, reading their body language, dissecting their facial expressions, and studying their choices of clothing. I was fascinated by how they interacted with the world around them and analyzed what it told me about who they were. My interest in picking up on people's emotions and reading deeper into their issues has assisted me in helping many women get to the core of their problems, take the next step, and open those doors to shifting into living joyous lives. However, this is not something I used to think of as a passion.

What you are passionate about is often not what you have been taught is acceptable or appropriate. We get so distracted by our hormones, planning out the events in our lives, and setting goals for the future that we forget about being ourselves. Later in life, if we end up on our own, we have to dig through a mountain of built-up emotional trauma to remember who we really are.

We don't know how to start over and move forward. Why do you think the self-help section in bookstores has expanded so greatly over the last ten years? We put ourselves at the bottom of our own list of priorities. Other people—and their lists of demands—take precedence over our own happiness. So many women choose to stay in relationships that make them feel inadequate because they believe it is what is expected—instead of moving on and allowing both parties to do what brings them joy. We put our passions on the back burner because we have been taught they are not important— and soon they are all but forgotten, leaving us only with regrets.

Your passions drive you. They are nestled away in your subconscious and put away for safe keeping, but they are begging to explode out of you! Instead of rediscovering them, you search elsewhere for something (usually a guy) that you think will bring joy into your life. The expectation is that someone out there will bring happiness, which is usually the case when you meet someone and develop a love affair.

Oh—the wonderful feeling of being in love! No matter what you are doing, you can't get him out of your head. You are caught in the ecstasy of a whirlwind of pleasure and bliss ... and it's the most wonderful place in the world. Every day feels like a new adventure. You awake with anticipation to hear from him, and you can't wipe the smile off your face for the life of you! Suddenly you are more aware of your appearance, wanting to be seen as sexy and seductive. It is an amazing feeling to have someone sneak a peek at you, knowing they desire you and find you sexy. Their desire to hold, touch, and be with you—even to listen to your voice—is a wonderful feeling.

The first stage of love is perfect in the beginning—and then comes the second stage—romance—all thoughtful, gift giving, and full of attention. You and your new partner find joy in doing kind deeds for each other. This is the level of love that many of us long to keep burning throughout the course of the relationship. Unfortunately, it often dies once we get comfortable with each other and determine what our roles should be.

Passion is the third stage of love. This is an intense plateau in the relationship. It's the steamy part! At this point, the relationship will simmer down and end—or it will morph into the next level.

At this next level of the relationship, intimacy, you start to really get to know each other. This was where my first love affair, after marriage, really failed. We had many serious, intimate conversations about our dreams and desires. I thought he was hearing me as well as sharing his own. However, after a few months, it became apparent that—although he actually listened to what I was saying—he didn't *hear* much of what I was really sharing. I ended the relationship at this level. I could not see myself being committed to someone who only desired to know the outer me—without wanting to get to know who I really was.

When you finally commit to someone—and agree to ride out the rest of your lives together—you are in the commitment stage.

It's exciting to watch a relationship in its infancy: the thrill of being together, the joys of discovering each other's little quirks, plentiful sex, dining and dancing, meeting each other's friends. However, sometimes they crash once they pass this point. I understand why women might prefer to stay away from this love drama.

It's important for those who rush back into the dating scene—looking for Mr. Right—to only do so if they are first happy with who and where they are in their lives. Otherwise, before the relationship even gets started, it is conditional. Relationships built on a set of conditions either don't last long or end up in shambles down the road. The secret is to be that which you want to attract. If you define Mr. Right as trustworthy, lovable, generous, and positive, then it is your duty to exude those qualities on every level (emotionally, mentally, physically, and spiritually).

People are always attracted to those with similar spirits and intentions. If you make it your quest to project that which you want to attract from another, soon you will see amazing results begin to actualize in your life experiences. Live every day using your emotions as guidance. When you know what feels right for you at all times, you cannot help but live passionately—and this will be the driving force in your life. Once you can do this, you are living consciously, choosing to live from your own beliefs and definitions—instead of everyone else's.

Have you ever heard a man say, "I want a woman with her own desires and goals—one who can stand on her own two feet"? He is talking about passion. Most men don't want to be the thing in a woman's life that is responsible for her happiness. Just as you do, they desire to enjoy a life of happiness with their partner.

An Aha Moment

One of my clients had an aha moment about the man factor. After breaking up with a man, she discovered that she began worrying about running out of money while living on her own. As soon as that familiar feeling started to take root, she found herself thinking about the need to have a man in her life. *Click! What was that? Did I just relate running out of money to needing a man?* Suddenly, it was all clear. Her culture dictated that the man's role was to provide security and take care of the woman. She associated the two very closely without even knowing it.

She had exposed this on her own by paying attention to her emotions. This was an unforgettable moment where she became aware of one of her nasty neural pathways (which I refer to as butt cords) and released a tie that was draining her electricity. She could also say she *unplugged* one of her core beliefs that she wasn't aware existed. The neural pathways are formed at a very early age. You may have adopted them from others as truths without giving thought to their meanings—or why you bought into them in the first place.

Figuring this out completely on her own and feeling that aha moment felt like uncovering a lost trinket of useful information (or a nice little hidden gem), and she was able to take her first step forward with renewed spirit. She felt empowered by her discovery. In these moments, you just *get* something. It clicks, and a breath of fresh air blows in, clearing out some of the fog you have grown accustomed to. It feels so good that you want to shout from the rooftops!

This is the perfect time to grab your journal and enter an aha moment you may have experienced. Go get your journal—or a piece of paper—and give it some thought *right now*. Aha moments can change your life. They are moments when you connect the dots about something that has troubled you. You may finally make sense of an event or situation and reveal a self-defeating pattern. Suddenly you get it and say, "Aha."

Recall all of the former love relationships in your life—and see if you can detect any patterns.

For example:

a) In my youth, I could never understand why I wasn't able to attract a nice guy.
b) One day I realized that I didn't feel worthy of a loving relationship.
c) The closest example I had to a loving relationship was my mother and father.
d) Bingo! As my father grew ill with heart disease, I felt pushed aside and unloved. I came to the conclusion that he didn't show me more affection because I was not a "good girl."
e) Feeling starved for attention—and being willing to do anything to get it—I chose to be bad. Being yelled at, after all, is attention too.
f) Bad girls don't have a good life. Time to bring on the bad boys!

Soon after this revelation, I attracted a man who was fun and young at heart. He brought out the best in me. This guy is my ex now, but he was the perfect man for me at that time.

Take the time to give some thought to what you have defined as failed relationships. What do you really believe is the root cause of these failures? Did you expect too much because too much was expected of you as you blossomed into womanhood? Were you overly critical because you were criticized? Did you set your sights too high or too low? Try to connect the dots. This is not an exercise in blame. How you decided to interpret another person's actions was simply a choice. Sit for a moment, consider your past relationships, and see if you can connect any dots.

Online Dating

Online dating has to be the biggest boom since social media started. I can't believe how many couples I have talked to who met online! I mean, it's huge! When I finally decided I was ready to date, it was all I heard about. I was already on the prowl, checking out every guy who caught my eye, looking for rings on fingers, evaluating whether they were my type, and getting a feel for what age I was most attracted to. I had no idea where or how I was going to meet single men. None of my friends were hopping on the "let me set you up" wagon I had heard so much about. When I kept seeing advertisements and hearing about these Internet dating sites, I decided to check them out.

If you have never engaged in online dating, you are probably wondering how it all works. You are presented with a database of eligible men who are searching for their new Miss Right, Miss Friend, or Miss Playmate. Take your time and peruse the men available in your area. See who catches your eye. Then dig in a little deeper and read some profiles. Get a feel for the entire online dating experience. The steps you choose to take with someone after you engage in an online conversation (meeting, chatting on the phone, etc.) are entirely up to you. However, don't let the need for security from another individual compel you to make any rash decisions. Don't get clingy and immediately put all of your eggs in one basket—give your power away—and tie yourself to a guy because you are worried you may never meet anyone. Settling is never a good option.

A ton of Internet dating sites are ready to add you into their list of available women for men to explore. Which one do you choose, and how do you do this Internet dating thing?

- **Step One:** Decide what kind of relationship you are looking for. Get real with yourself. When I first started dating, I wanted to play the field and date with no real attachments. Are you interested in casual dating, friendships only, friendships that may lead to dating, adult dating, or are you looking for something that will eventually lead to a commitment?

- **Step Two:** Get your pretty butt over to a computer and search "online dating sites." Make a list or bookmark the ones you find.

- **Step Three:** Look at what the dating services have to offer—and decide which ones meet your needs. If you are not sure which one to check out first, select a familiar one. Keep a record of how much each charges—and what they provide. You don't want to join several sites and get caught up in paying too many fees!

- **Step Four:** Take advantage of any that offer free registration (most do), and take a peek around. Get a feel for how the site works. Some will engineer searches for you and play matchmaker. You might prefer to be in charge of generating your own searches. Would you enjoy having both options?

- **Step Five:** Have a friend take a few digital pictures of you and help you upload them to your profiles. Do not use old pictures of you with your ex (wedding pictures are a no-no). Do not post group shots where onlookers will have no clue which person is actually you. Do not even consider eighties glam shots as a good illustration of how you look today!

- **Step Six:** Fill out a few profiles to get a feel for what is required. Almost everyone struggles in this area. However, if you are seriously ready to date and like this online process, are actually looking for a committed relationship, and need help with this part, I can hook you up with my preferred dating coach. E-mail me at meandmypassions@gmail.com.

- **Step Seven:** Start communicating. Many women freak out here. Before you start chatting with any of these guys online, be prepared to be asked to meet. Yes! You have to meet them in real life! Choose a meeting place that is comfortable for you. I chose the café in my favorite bookstore as a meeting place. I felt safe meeting in public. If we chose to have a more intimate conversation later, there was a restaurant nearby. The first component of this step is chatting online. You can exchange text messages through most dating sites. Remember to be mindful when communicating. Do not to take what you read too seriously. When I met the man I am now dating on eHarmony, I didn't get his subtle jokes at first. It can be hard to pick up on the delivery of something in a chat window or an e-mail.

After a week of interacting with these sites, you will get a feel for which ones you like best—and where to invest your time and money.

Tip:
People who choose to pay more than $40 per month are more serious about coordinating an offline date.

Online dating can be an enjoyable way to meet men—as long as you are truly ready to do so and don't have expectations that are too high.

What Kind of Guy Is the Right Guy for Me?

How would *you* define the perfect man? What words would you use to describe him? In your journal, write down any that feel like a match for you. If there is a quality not listed, add it to your list.

Mature—Kind—Honest—Loves Dancing—Makes Me Laugh—Sexual—Appreciative—Healthy—Active—Wealthy—Adventurous—Animal Lover—Innovative—Successful—Great Cook—Manly—Seasoned—Giving—Simple—Romantic—Faithful—Dependable—Intelligent—Generous—A Good Listener—Stylish—Open Minded—Relaxed—Good Conversationalist—Loves to Travel—Intellectual—Enjoys Shopping—Likes Technology—Has a Specific Religion—Loves the Outdoors—Young at Heart—Financially Secure—Animal Lover—Loves the City—Loves the Country—Spiritual—Social—Family Man—Tentative—Handyman—Protective—Motivated—Committed—Reliable

You now have a list of characteristics you would like in your next mate. More than a list of ten characteristics is too long. Evaluate your list of man expectations carefully, and choose ones that feel like deal breakers. Which qualities really matter to you, and in what ways are you willing to open your heart to the possibility that something amazing and perfect will show up?

Packing light does not mean setting your expectations too low. I'm not asking you to shorten your list so that you won't be disappointed. What you should have is a more general list of expectations and fewer specific ones. It is my desire that you use this *list* exercise to get real with yourself about what you expect from a partner. As I said earlier, having an actual list is not a good idea.

The next step is to define what these traits mean to you. When we define these characteristics, our subconscious (ego) draws on past experiences, usually negative ones, to come to conclusions. A great cook could be on your list because you were the main cook in your last relationship, and you don't want this position any longer. I don't enjoy cooking and want someone to feed me great food. Yum! Is it a deal breaker?

How about adventurous? Do you mean he desires to travel the world—or he likes to go on fun, romantic outings with you? Why would you choose faithful? Have you experienced unfaithfulness or are worried this might be a possibility? The characteristics we choose are related to events we would probably rather forget.

The qualities you want in a lover may show up in your life, but not as you expect. Let's say you would adore a man who loves to sing. Maybe you enjoy karaoke, would love a man to sing to you, or want someone to sing with. You might connect with a man who loves singing, but he feels more like a friend than a lover. Perhaps you become good friends who enjoy singing together, and he introduces you to a friend who you are attracted to. Sometimes what we desire shows up in different ways. You now have a friend you can sing with and a possible romance.

Making a list of the aspects you want in a new lover—and getting clear on your definitions and deal breakers—is an enlightening process. Finding a mate typically starts on a more physical level; physical attraction comes first. As you've matured, you may have become more aware of your desires in a mate, especially after a long relationship. It is valuable to have a clear definition of those desires.

How does defining the ideal qualities you want in a mate ensure that they are even going to show up? What authority do you have over who you meet? When you have a clear understanding of what you want, you yourself can be that which you desire. We all know that like attracts like. People with similar interests always flock together. This is also true when you want to attract a lover. If you can be all of the character traits on your *man expectation list*, then you will attract that which you desire. When you create a list that is too long, what you really desire gets buried. It's also not a good idea to put all of your hopes into a new guy, expecting he will fit your long list. Remember, it's not up to him to make you happy.

Women often throw themselves out there, hoping someone will want them. They can also be defensive and set in their ways. They have the attitude that men better accept them for who they are because they are not going to change! This is not a good foundation. This is not a good place to start. When you know what you want, you *become* what you want and can remain focused on your true desires.

When I first chose to start dating, I had a conscious list of man expectations I thought were important to me. My first list looked something like this:

- Deal breakers: Hunting and camping. Not my things whatsoever!
- He is open-minded.
- He has similar interests, but he will have some interesting things to teach me, which I will enjoy.
- Deal breaker: He is spiritual versus religious.
- He can be up to ten years my senior or three years younger.
- He is taller than I am. The taller, the better. I love tall men.
- He is sexually active and wants to explore our sexuality together.
- He is financially secure.
- He is generous.
- He loves to travel.
- He has a pleasant body.
- He likes to have fun.

Those were my top requests. Can you see where I was somewhat vague in my definitions? What did I mean by open-minded? What undisclosed plans did I really have in mind? Can you see how this was not the best place to start?

When I decided to check out the Internet dating sites to see what kind of men were on them, I knew I wasn't ready for a committed relationship. The intention I had was more like window-shopping, but I was ready if someone wanted to meet in person. I had my mental list and was ready to go.

The first guy I started a conversation with was too over the top for me. Within a few messages, he was talking like we were already in a steady relationship. He told me how much he hated when women stayed in touch with their exes. I could tell that this comment was due to a lot of heartbreak. Poor fellow! Since my relationship with my ex was good, I chose to stop the connection. He had met some of my expectations. He was older, taller, attractive, ran his own business, and loved to travel. He just wasn't for me.

I continued chatting with other eligible bachelors who I found quite interesting. Take a look at how my list of man expectations evolved as I began meeting them in person.

Bachelor #1 was a truck driver. He was polite and pleasant—and totally broke due to his divorce. I felt guilty that I was allowing this money deal breaker to stop me from pursuing him. We eventually went on a date—and he informed me he had herpes. I wasn't sure how to handle this information; since the relationship hadn't really begun, I let it go.

My girlfriend didn't approve of him because she believed he hadn't grown up yet. She came to this conclusion because he collected movie figurines. To her, this was little boy stuff—not something a grown man should be doing. This was not my point of view at all, and I did my best to explain how some people collect models in the same way she collects books. She had made up her mind that men like this had not grown up and were immature.

From this first encounter, I subconsciously tweaked my list and moved having money up to the top and added not having any sexual diseases. But he was in fact, older, taller, open-minded, and a great conversationalist.

Bachelor #2 and I had some great conversations online. It appeared we had a lot in common. We met for coffee at my usual spot, and I instantly loved his voice. He was taller, pleasant looking, and had a good job. Tick those off the list. After talking over coffee, we decided to move our conversation to the restaurant for a glass of wine.

We had a fantastic evening of conversation (another tick), and before parting ways, I kissed him deeply, even though his teeth were not the pearly white I usually admired. After that first kiss, he was totally smitten. In the days to follow, he phoned and e-mailed me regularly. When we talked on the phone, he asked why I hadn't answered the questions he asked in his e-mails. I felt he was accusing me of hiding something. To top it off, he was a sloppy kisser. I almost needed a towel after a few kisses—not a turn-on for me at all. I just wasn't into him as much as he was into me, and that relationship also ended rather abruptly.

I tweaked my list again and added good teeth—and being a good kisser! I also decided that I did not want a relationship with anyone who lived close by because they could show up at any time—and I don't like those kinds of surprises. I certainly wasn't ready for that much attachment.

Bachelor #3 was rather unique. His profile stated that he lived in London, but he had actually moved up north to get into a business. This impressed me. *Finally a guy who at least had something going for him.* The problem was that he was thirteen hours away! He was a deep thinker, and we had similar interests. He made a point that we talk every day. He was tall, bald, and his arms were covered with tattoos. The bad boy of my past had appeared, and I was head over heels. Many of us have a type we fall for who is all wrong for us but we can't walk away from.

After much discussion, we decided I would go up north to meet him and stay for a week. I traveled thirteen hours to meet a strange man, simply to find love. Our first day together was wonderful, filled with long walks, cooking, and sex. Then the bomb dropped. My pattern of attracting drug addicts and alcoholics had manifested again. On top of this, he was extremely controlling. If he felt something I was saying was negative in any way, he would literally pinch me—and tell me to think about what I had said. He used pain to enforce his disapproval.

By the third day, I desperately wanted to leave. I couldn't believe I had driven thirteen hours to date a guy I had met on the Internet! Was I out of my mind? Yes, I was! Oh, more tweaking of that list.

Are you scared of taking a leap and finding out what kinds of men are waiting for you on Internet dating sites? I hope not. Remember that these are my experiences—not yours. I have met many happily married couples who met online. Don't let my stories scare you. You simply need to get in touch with what you want in a relationship— and then know he is out there. My list continued to evolve after each encounter, and I took a step back on how much I was willing to risk to meet these men. I now knew addictions, of any sort, were a deal breaker, and that an hour away was far enough.

Bachelor #4! This guy met most of my expectations. He appeared to be open-minded, enjoyed dancing, wine, hanging at the beach, and shopping. He didn't have ex issues and had varying tastes in friends—from Average Joes to those who were more upper class. I admired how he could fit into both worlds and enjoy them equally. Money issues were also a nonissue. My desire for someone with great teeth had showed up too!

People are usually on their best behavior during the first three months of a relationship. It was at about this time that I noticed him using control and disapproval as a ploy to keep people he loved safe. Plus, on two occasions, he accused me of hiding a fictitious lover. I do admit that I love admiring men. Being the people watcher I am, it's bound to happen, and I require a partner who isn't bothered by this. With 3.8 billion men on the planet, it's quite difficult not to look at some of them. But I am a loyal, one-man woman.

We dated for almost eight months before I called it off. I was cutting off too much of who I really am to fit into his world. I felt he wanted a wife to stay at home and look after him, and I had glorious plans for my future. We just didn't fit, and I chose to cut it off.

By now I was becoming very clear about what I really wanted in a relationship with a man. My list now looked something like this:

- allows me to be all of who I am
- adores and appreciates me, and I adore and appreciate him back
- open-minded and willing to embrace new ways of thinking
- good hygiene
- healthy and sexually active
- financially secure
- willing to be a best friend and a lover
- wants to travel the world with me
- clean-cut, my height or taller, and pleasant to my eyes
- doesn't live in the same city

What is so exhilarating about consciously paying attention to what you think and how you feel during the dating process causes you to shift from reacting to situations to responding to them. Once this begins to happen, you become clear about your true desires.

Bachelor #5. He loved to have fun. Although he did fit many of my expectations, the main topic of conversation with this guy was sex, including how long he liked it to last, a list of his sexual preferences, women he had sex with and what he didn't like about them, and how large his member was. Everything we talked about led back to sex. I should have paid attention to this red flag. I'm a pretty sexual woman and am not afraid to explore my desires, but this much discussion on one subject was excessive. I went on a few dates with him, but sex was always given too much attention. In his defense, he was looking for Miss Playmate—and not Miss Right. When Bachelor #6 showed up, I was happy to move on.

Bachelor #6 met all of my desires. We met at my usual spot for our first date, and when he walked in, it was me who was smitten. He was tall and adorable, and he had a sexy voice and a great laugh. We shared a bottle of wine at the nearby restaurant and stayed until closing. We were completely comfortable with each other from the moment we locked eyes. We are coming up on six months together, and I am extremely pleased with how we are progressing.

By the time this man showed up, I had become quite clear with my expectations and had finally created the foundation I needed to have a relationship. All that I desired, I could be. I also let go of being so attached to any outcome. I knew what really worked for me and knew it was possible for it to show up in my life. This knowing state of mind is magical. Being in a state of knowing taps you into the power of positive expectation. I knew what was really important to me, and I just knew it was possible, which is always more expansive and joyful.

Don't be afraid to put yourself out there. Approach the man factor with a new perspective—without any limiting expectations. Create new relationship paths instead of following what is familiar to you. Trust in yourself. It's not fun for either party if you try to fit into each other's lives. It can be exhausting! Take a playful approach. You are seasoned to perfection—with so many wonderful experiences waiting for you. Man or no man, you've got a huge future ahead of you—and you are amazing!

Chapter Fourteen
INNER PIECE

The change you create in your life is a gift. I encourage you to reread this book in a month or two and play with the exercises again. Continue to set new, fun, positive adventures in motion. A wonderful way to look at where you currently are is by imagining you have completed one puzzle—and are starting a new one. It's like that feeling of putting in the last piece of a puzzle. *It's done. Whew! That was a lot of work. Some areas were super easy and just fell into place. Others were almost impossible. But I did it!*

Imagine that you are beginning a new puzzle. The atmosphere of this puzzle is completely different. It's critical to remember, discover, redefine, and find happiness where you are right now. What is the first step when starting a new puzzle? Finding all the edge pieces and building your foundation.

Creating the foundation releases you from the past; you embrace what's new and unfamiliar in front of you. You are creating a space that reflects your inner goddess. You are remembering your passions. You are discovering new ways to play with the joy that surrounds you, and you are practicing keeping an open mind. Your foundation is who you really are. It's *the you* who is happy with who you are—and doesn't mind spending time with yourself. It's *the you* who is happy first—and doesn't expect someone or something else to provide happiness.

Building a puzzle is not a rushed process. Instead, you get comfortable, enjoy a beverage, and settle in for a few hours of puzzling. You relax and let it unfold. When you begin to get frustrated, you walk away and return when you are in a better state of mind. In your life right now, you are getting settled, flipping the pieces over, and starting fresh. Stop fighting and trying to micromanage all the pieces into place.

Set your foundation—and get excited about how the rest is going to come together. It's going to be so much fun! You've done this before; it's simply a different picture. There could be tough parts in this new puzzle that will seem exciting in the beginning—but they might frustrate you later. Once you give yourself permission to flow with the process, you will come back relaxed and ready to dig in again. Everything will work out perfectly. You will be astonished by how some of these new experiences will snap into place easily. Others may require more effort.

Everything you desire comes from *within*. No one and nothing out there can make your struggles go away. When you feel vulnerable, utilize the guidance of the people in your life. You are the final piece of your puzzle. All of the good stuff comes from within you.

I hope I have helped you become more aware of who you are so you can embrace this newfound singledom—as I did. Relax and take your time. Don't expect so much from yourself. Embrace the inner you and your inner piece.

Thank you for allowing me to share my stories, insights, coaching tips, tools, and techniques while you are in this space and creating more. You are welcome to visit me at meandmypassions.com to sign up for my newsletter, register for a TeleWebSeries, check out my coaching packages, or read my blog.

EPILOGUE

Since the completion of *RedeFIND SiNGLE 40+,* I have expanded even more as an individual. I am happy to share that I continue to coach women by helping them unplug from everywhere they are limiting themselves from their electrifying genius potential. I continue to help other coaches, spiritual teachers, authors, and healers create teleclasses, and me&my Passions (www.meandmypassions.com) is a thriving business and allowing me to inspire even more women to greatness. Bachelor #6 and I have been together for almost two years, and we are still madly in love. When you line up the energy of one part of your life, the rest follows along.

I would love the opportunity to help you expand as you remember yourself and rediscover your passions.

I am KiCKASS iNTUiTiVE Life Coach Catherine.

Visit me at www.meandmypassions.com or

e-mail me at meandmypassions@gmail.com.